"Some books are written from
experience. Bob Burton comb
helpful book. The footnote cita
but his own experience in loc;
tested realism to his writing. I have been encouraged and challenged by this
work. You will be as well!"

—**Timothy K. Beougher**, Billy Graham Professor of Evangelism,
associate dean, Billy Graham School of Missions, Evangelism
and Ministry, The Southern Baptist Theological Seminary

"Bob Burton has captured the essence of a church on mission. It is not about what the church dreams up to do for God, but what God chooses to do through a local church. I have known Bob for many years and have always appreciated his passion for the Church and God's plan to use it to transform the world."

—**Henry Blackaby**, founder, Blackaby Ministries International

"I'm grateful for this incredibly well-written and power-packed book. It is a gift to the church. Today more than ever the church needs to understand and embrace the truth that Bob systematically lays forth in this book—the truth about the activity of God and the role of the church in that activity. I eagerly commend this book to you. I know it will be a valuable resource in your library."

—**Mark Clifton**, senior director, Church Replanting,
North American Mission Board

"The Spiritual DNA of a Church on Mission is a welcome resource for pastors seeking to lead their congregations to accomplish the mission of Jesus to 'seek and to save the lost'. This book has both passion and a plan. [With] the integration of small group study in Acts, prayer strategy, Bible reading plan, sermon helps, and contemporary stories[,] readers fully immerse themselves in the early church in Acts. I wholeheartedly recommend this book for those who want to experience God's touch upon their church and community."

—**Andre' Dobson**, senior pastor, Calvary Baptist Church, Alton, IL

"Burton draws on years of involvement in the church planting movement in North America. He is a seasoned veteran and a walking encyclopedia of knowledge. This book is a must-read to get a good grasp on our genetic roots, and an understanding of how God has wired and imbedded his DNA in the 21st-century North American church."

—**Sam Douglass**, director of unreached, unengaged people groups
and new countries, Dynamic Church Planting International

"Missional drift destroys effectiveness, hurts morale, erodes unity and eventually causes people to question whether an organization even needs to exist. This is the risk so many churches face as they are drawn to 'good' activities that ultimately distract from their primary mission. Burton has put the on-mission church under a microscope, and he unpacks the key elements that must be present if we are to stay on target with the mission Jesus gave."

—**Kevin Ezell**, president, North American Mission Board

"*The Spiritual DNA of a Church on Mission* combines historical data with scriptural counsel and recommended best practices. Bob takes into account the seismic demographic shift in America and gives solid biblical advice that every church needs to hear and heed. Every church leader looking to make an impact on their community needs to read this book."

—**Mark Hearn**, pastor, First Baptist Church, Duluth, GA

"*The Spiritual DNA of a Church on Mission* is a must-read for the American pastor and missionary. It is written from conviction and personal experience. You will be blessed!"

—**Neal Hughes**, director of missions, Montgomery Baptist Association

"Bob Burton has proven to be a valuable asset in today's Kingdom work. As a pastor he has experienced the challenges that every local church faces, and as a church planting specialist for the North American Mission Board he has successfully navigated uncharted waters. I am convinced that *The Spiritual DNA of a Church on Mission* will help existing churches recommit and refocus on the task of reaching the lost as well as influence new churches to start with priorities and practices that will produce fruit immediately. This is a 'how-to' book that actually tells you how to do it. Do not start another project or ministry unless you have read it."

—**Johnny Hunt**, senior vice president of evangelism and leadership, North American Mission Board, pastor, First Baptist Church, Woodstock, GA, and former president, the Southern Baptist Convention

"*The Spiritual DNA of a Church on Mission* hits at the heart of what North America and the world need: renewal and spiritual awakening. I am particularly pleased by this work's emphasis on prayer, without which we can never do all that God asks us to do. Even if you differ at points with this book, you will come out with a genuine desire for God to do something mighty in and through your church."

—**Chuck Lawless**, vice president, spiritual formation and ministry centers, dean, doctoral studies, professor, evangelism and missions, Southeastern Baptist Theological Seminary, and team leader, theological education strategists, International Mission Board.

"In *The Spiritual DNA of a Church on Mission*, Burton challenges the local church to rediscover and freshly apply mission principles by fully immersing themselves in the book of Acts. God has faithfully written the 'script' for His followers. The Holy Scriptures instruct, guide, inform and inspire us to live according to our God-given spiritual missionary DNA. Bob is pointing us to that script."

—**Fred Luter Jr.** pastor, Franklin Avenue Baptist Church, New Orleans, LA, and former president, the Southern Baptist Convention

"A biblical and practical guide! Burton does a wonderful job describing healthy characteristics of the church. But he does not stop there. Beginning with Scripture and transitioning to contemporary examples and action steps, he takes us from the theoretical and moves to reality. No armchair expert here. Learn from this work, but apply it for the glory of God among the nations."

—**J. D. Payne**, associate professor of Christian ministry, Samford University

"In the New Testament, we discover that the local church was born to join in God's global mission. Bob Burton clearly understands this reality and provides a fresh look at the early church's participation in God's kingdom activity as revealed in the pages of the book of Acts. His practical unpacking of *The Spiritual DNA of a Church on Mission* is a phenomenal resource for any church longing to greater understand its role in God's glorious mission."

—**Vance Pitman**, senior pastor, Hope Church, Las Vegas, NV

"In his DNA-themed book and workbook, Burton has passionately and creatively called the church to rediscover the first-century church in Acts. He has captured just how an immersion in the book of Acts will change the missional culture of a church. If you and your church apply the ten spiritual DNA principles expressed by the first-century churches, then you will be in a position to experience the transformation that only God can give through the power of the Holy Spirit. Read this book and discover your God-given missionary DNA."

—**Bobby Sena**, assistant professor of ministry, director, Hispanic DMin, Midwestern Baptist Theological Seminary

"Too often our churches are dry deserts, parched by the selfishness and consumerism plaguing modern Christianity. Bob shows us that the book of Acts contains everything our congregations need to develop a missions lifestyle. *The Spiritual DNA of a Church on Mission* provides an extensive biblical foundation, as well as helpful insights and practical suggestions to help your church reclaim its missionary DNA."

—**Sandy Wisdom-Martin**, executive director-treasurer, Woman's Missionary Union

Rediscovering the 1st Century Church
for 21st Century
Spiritual Awakening

The
SPIRITUAL DNA
of a
CHURCH ON MISSION

BOB BURTON

WORDSEARCH
ACADEMIC

NASHVILLE, TENNESSEE

The Spiritual DNA of a Church on Mission
Copyright © 2020 by Bob Burton

Published by Wordsearch® Academic, an imprint of B&H Academic
Nashville, Tennessee

All rights reserved.

ISBN: 978-1-4336-4587-7

Dewey Decimal Classification: 261.1
Subject Heading: CHURCH / MISSIONS / CHURCH WORK

Except where noted, all scriptures have been taken from the Christian Standard Bible®, Copyright © 2017 by Holman Bible Publishers. Used by permission. Christian Standard Bible® and CSB® are federally registered trademarks of Holman Bible Publishers.

Scripture quotations marked KJV have been taken from the King James Version. Public domain.

The web addresses referenced in this book were live and correct at the time of the book's publication but may be subject to change.

Cover design and illustration by Darren Welch.

Printed in the United States of America

1 2 3 4 5 6 7 8 9 10 • 25 24 23 22 21 20

To Dana, my wife.
Next to Jesus, she is my best friend in this life and my fellow traveler on this journey of spiritual DNA discovery.

CONTENTS

Acknowledgments xi
Preface xv
Introduction. 1

Chapter 1	Spiritual Preparation: Wait, Pray, and Expect God to Work (Jerusalem). 9
Chapter 2	Spiritual Authority: Rely on the Holy Spirit's Power (Jerusalem) 25
Chapter 3	Spiritual Understanding: Focus on Peoples and Places (Jerusalem/Caesarea) 39
Chapter 4	Spiritual Leadership: Identify and Nurture Missional Leaders (Antioch) 53
Chapter 5	Spiritual Synergy: Work Together for Greater Impact (Philippi). 67
Chapter 6	Spiritual Receptivity: Discover Persons of Peace (Philippi). . . .79
Chapter 7	Spiritual Sowing: Evangelize and Make Disciples (Thessalonica/Berea) 95
Chapter 8	Spiritual Bridges: Leverage Points of Connection (Athens). . .111
Chapter 9	Spiritual Giftedness: Gather and Give Resources from the Harvest (Corinth) 127

Chapter 10 Spiritual Warfare: Fight the Good Fight (Ephesus)......... 145

Chapter 11 A Church in Action: Personalize the Spiritual
DNA Principles................................... 163

Afterword: The Next Act for You and Your Church 169

Appendix 1: Preview of *The Spiritual DNA of a Church
on Mission Workbook* 175

Appendix 2: The Spiritual DNA Principles and Churches in Acts 177

Appendix 3: The Spiritual DNA Principles in the Life of Christ......... 179

Appendix 4: The Spiritual DNA Principles in the Missionary Discourses.. 181

Appendix 5: The Spiritual DNA Principles as Modern Mutations 183

Appendix 6: The Spiritual DNA Principles in the Church at Philippi 185

Appendix 7: The Spiritual DNA Principles in the Parables............. 187

Appendix 8: The Spiritual DNA Principles in Awakenings and Revivals
of North America................................... 191

Appendix 9: The Spiritual DNA Principles in Entrepreneurship......... 193

About the Author.. 195

Name and Subject Index 197

Scripture Index.. 201

ACKNOWLEDGMENTS

On my desk are several sticky notes with meaningful quotes and Bible verses that have served to guide and encourage me as I worked on *The Spiritual DNA of a Church on Mission* and *The Spiritual DNA of a Church on Mission Workbook*. Almost every time I sat down to write, I reviewed them.

One that stands out is from the author Robert Frost who said, "No tears in the writer no tears in the reader." For a man who doesn't cry much, I must confess there were times of tears for me. There were times I sensed God's presence while writing that brought me to a place of grateful tears for the Holy Spirit's work. There were times when discovering a quote or insight would bring tears of joy for God's grace in helping me. There were times when there were tears of battle, sensing the spiritual warfare going on in my heart and soul while writing this book. There were a few times late at night when there were tears from simply straining my eyes with too much screen time. But when I begin to think of the people who have spoken into my life, there are tears on another level.

I'd like to start with abundant thanks to Dana, my wife, who, next to Jesus, is the love of my life. Without her support, you would not hold this book in your hands. My three boys: Andy, Noah, and Luke, along with their lovely wives delight me as a dad and have faithfully encouraged me. Of course, my grandson, Willie, gave me a much-needed break from writing to play like only a "Paw Paw" can.

Acknowledgments

Thanks to my friend K. C. Crino. God used him to spark a new passion in me for the book of Acts. My deepest appreciation to Chuck Lawless, the first person with whom I shared my concept of the spiritual DNA of the churches in Acts. He encouraged me to pursue this and, as one of my advisors, walked me through the project in doctoral form. Likewise, thanks to Henry Blackaby, who told me to "get it right" and figuratively looked over my shoulder with those words throughout this writing. Special thanks to my professors Michael Wilder, Larry Purcell, Hal Pettegrew, Gary Fangmann, J. D. Payne, Gary Bredfelt, and my doctoral cohort group from The Southern Baptist Theological Seminary, all of whom God used to shape this project in its early development. One friend in particular, Clip Suddeth from my cohort group, has gone above and beyond to assist me in seeing this book to completion. Again, thank you so much.

Another group of trusted advisors reviewed early chapters of this book and provided insightful comments: Clip Suddeth, Dave Howeth, Kerry Jackson, Neal Hughes, Ray Willis, Andre Dobson, John Horn, Dave Evans, Tiffany Smith, Robbey Smith, Monty Mullenix, Phil Miglioratti, Scott Westrum, Jeff Calloway, Codi Wiltshire, Steve Howell, Larry Rhodes, and Charlie Ferhman. All of you brought your own unique life view, expertise, and experiences to make this a better work.

My colleagues at the North American Mission Board are family and I'm so thankful for their influence in my life and ministry since 2001. Special thanks go to our president, Kevin Ezell, who has led us well, made me laugh with his quick wit, and spoken into my life on numerous occasions. Thank you for encouraging me in this work. My prayer is this book will move people from pews to action.

Thanks also to my publishing team from Wordsearch Academic, starting with Jim Baird and Chris Thompson who believed in the value of the work and gave a first-time author an opportunity. Likewise, a very special thanks to Sarah Landers, who was my project coordinator; to Renee Chavez, who served as project manager, and to Kristin Goble of PerfecType, who took these manuscripts from their raw state and produced two beautifully designed books. Lastly, I'd like to express my sincere gratitude to Jennifer Day, who served as my writing coach and helped me see this book to the finish line.

There is one last sticky note from my desk I want to mention. I wrote Ps 96:7–9 on this one and circled the word *ascribe*. It is my heartfelt and fervent prayer that any good that comes to the kingdom as a result of this book would truly "ascribe" glory to God.

> ***Ascribe*** *to the* L<small>ORD</small>*, you families of the peoples,* ***ascribe*** *to the* L<small>ORD</small> *glory and strength.* ***Ascribe*** *to the* L<small>ORD</small> *the glory of his name; bring an offering and enter his courts. Worship the* L<small>ORD</small> *in the splendor of his holiness; let the whole earth tremble before him.*

To God be the glory!

PREFACE

My journey with the book of Acts began as a new church-planting catalyst with the North American Mission Board. My friend and missionary mentor K. C. Crino challenged me with this life-changing advice: "Read the book of Acts. Become a student of that book because everything you really need to know about missions and church planting is found there."

Taking this advice seriously, I immersed myself in the study of Acts. As I did so, I quickly realized the spiritual DNA of the church in Acts was not reflected in many contemporary churches. Something was seriously wrong.

One day in a conversation with Henry Blackaby, author of *Experiencing God*, he straightforwardly reminded me that Acts 1:8 is an announcement, not a programmatic strategy. The red-letter announcement is that God's mission force is made up of powerful, Holy Spirit-filled witnesses who are commanded to take the message here, there, and everywhere. In *The Experiencing God Study Bible*, Henry asks some penetrating questions about Acts: Is God's mission the number one priority in our lives? Are we willing to go anywhere and do whatever God wants on mission for him? Are we willing to make adjustments in our lifestyle for God's mission?[1]

These conversations and questions prompted my own questions: What might happen if individual Christians and local churches truly became

---

[1] Henry Blackaby, *The Experiencing God Study Bible: The Bible for Knowing and Doing the Will of God* (Nashville: B&H, 1994), 1600.

immersed in the book of Acts and "got it right" as the early followers did? What would happen if individual Christians and local churches began to express our true spiritual DNA instead of suppressing it? If this were to happen, I confidently believe we would see a church that looks like the book of Acts. It is this reality that continues to motivate me to be a missionary change agent—calling the church back to be equipped and mobilized to God's mission. The modern church needs this message urgently.

Let me ask you: Do you believe an unprecedented move of God and a spiritual awakening in North America is even possible in the twenty-first century? I believe God is sovereignly more than able to grant it during this time and season in history. Last year, I heard motivational speaker and marketing consultant Simon Sinek make a statement that God used to confirm my seventeen-year journey in writing this book. He said, "Start with the Why. Few people or organizations know why they do what they do." He then drew three circles with "why" in the center circle, "what" in the inner ring, and "how" in the outer ring. He called it the Golden Circle.[2] In my observation, the pressing need of the hour is for all of us—pastors, leaders, teachers, and believers—to first know *why* we do what we do, determine *what* is to be done, and then learn practical tools and a process for *how* to do it.

In my assignment with the Send Network (North American Mission Board), God has called me to help equip and mobilize the church to be on mission. I assist churches in taking their next missional step so more lost people can hear and respond to the gospel. *That's my "why."*

The "Why" of this book is merely an extension of my mission. Most twenty-first-century churches are in desperate need of revival. Our continent is in need of spiritual awakening like no other time in history. There are lost

---

[2] Simon Sinek, *Start with the Why: How Great Leaders Inspire Everyone to Take Action* (New York: Penguin, 2009), 3:37–51. Also, view the video from Sinek for his perspective on the importance of the "Why." Simon Sinek, "How Great Leaders Inspire Action," TED talk, September 2005, https://www.ted.com/talks/simon_sinek_how_great_leaders_inspire_action.

people without Christ who are simply not ready for heaven and this generation has a responsibility to bring the hope of Christ to these lost people.

The "What" of this book is to help us rediscover and experience the ten life-changing biblical principles of the book of Acts in our own lives—to learn what an everyday Christ follower and a church on mission really looks like. We cannot assume the average church knows what they should do because these biblical principles are often twisted from what they were intended to be.

The "How" of this book is creating a missional culture in our life and the life of our church through implementing the framework of seven cultural change factors. These are addressed and provided for you in the supplemental resource entitled *The Spiritual DNA of a Church on Mission Workbook*. The book and workbook together provide a holistic, integrated approach to experiencing a season of revival in your life and the life of your church through immersion in Acts.

Missionary mentors/coaches challenge and encourage everyday Christ followers and churches to be on mission. My desire is to be a missionary mentor/coach for you and your church. The tools in these two books are designed to give you a plan of action leading to spiritual awakening both individually and corporately, ultimately overflowing in your mission field. They are not meant to be a simplistic answer for complex problems. These books do not diminish the vocational office of a missionary, or tinker with the structures of the church, or even a call for an exact replication of the book of Acts events. These books are also not a list of prescriptive solutions from Acts, nor are they attempts to clone the first century church.[3]

---

[3] Scott Andrews, "The Use of the Term 'DNA' as a Missiological Metaphor in Contemporary Church Narratives," *HTS Teologiese Studies/Theological Studies* 72, no. 2 (September 2016): a3451, http://dx.doi.org/10.4102/hts.v72i2.3451. There are a few helpful spiritual DNA metaphors in contemporary authorship. Andrews calls attention to them. My emphasis as noted is to remain biblical-principle based and missional, and to intentionally stay in the spirit of Paul, who used the human body as a metaphor for the church—the body of Christ.

Instead, these books are a heartfelt and mindful call to us all to express the same principles Jesus modeled, taught, and infused in the life of his church. My prayerful desire is to see God initiate multiple small movements in local churches across North America that become one large, contagious movement of spiritual awakening which in turn changes the entire spiritual landscape for the sake of his glory.

INTRODUCTION

*For whatever was written in the past was written for our
instruction, so that we may have hope through endurance
and through the encouragement from the Scriptures.*
—Romans 15:4

*There exists in every church something that sooner or later works
against the very purpose for which it came into existence. So we
must strive very hard, by the grace of God, to keep the church
focused on the mission that Christ originally gave to it.*
—Will Vaus, *A Guide to the Thought of C. S. Lewis*

DNA discovery changes everything!

Do you remember the movie *Jurassic Park*? Michael Crichton's story centered on an ambitious science project-turned-theme park that goes horribly wrong. Genetic engineers had devised a way to breed and hatch once-extinct dinosaurs using DNA from the extracted blood of a prehistoric mosquito. The plan was to create a tourist destination, but during construction and development, an employee was killed by one of the dinosaurs. The investors then demanded assurance that the park was safe and viable, and three experts are brought in for a final assessment. During their review, one of the park employees shuts the power off in attempted espionage and the captive dinosaurs escape, crushing innocent people as they run for their lives. It's quite a story. But notice it's rooted in rediscovering original DNA.

The main character in *Jurassic Park* is consultant Dr. Ian Malcolm, one of the three experts invited to assess the park. Early on the scientist prophetically states, "The kind of control you are attempting is not possible. If there's one thing the history of evolution has taught us, it's that life will not be contained. Life breaks free. It expands to new territories. It crashes through barriers painfully, maybe even dangerously, . . . life finds a way."[1] Set aside the fiction and evolutionary fallacy of *Jurassic Park* for a moment and focus on the passion of Dr. Malcolm's statement: "Life finds a way!" What if pastors, church leaders, and people in the pews embrace Malcolm's passion and proclaim the missional truth that, "The gospel of Jesus Christ is life and life breaks free! It expands to new territories! It crashes through barriers painfully, maybe even dangerously, but *God* finds a way!"? The early disciples experienced this. What would happen if we recovered their original DNA for the church?

In his primer lesson on DNA, educator Joe Hanson compares DNA to a detailed manual for building a person out of cells. His awe-inspiring TedEx video, entitled *DNA: The Book of You*, provides this definition: "Deoxyribonucleic acid (DNA) molecules are informational molecules encoding the genetic instructions used in the development and functioning of all known living organisms and many viruses."[2] In short, DNA is the basic building block of life. When we talk about the spiritual DNA of the church, we're referring to the basic building block—fundamentally missionary in character—that so powerfully exploded the growth of the early church. These are the DNA strands or principles the earliest disciples followed that resulted in an incredible move of God. My hope is that as we

---

[1] Michael Crichton, *Jurassic Park: A Novel* (New York: Random House-Ballantine Books, 1990), 178.

[2] "DNA: The Book of You," TED-Ed, accessed May 30, 2019, https://ed.ted.com/lessons/dna-the-book-of-you-joe-hanson#digdeeper.

walk through these DNA strands, we'll return to who we're meant to be both individually and corporately, and experience revival like we've never seen before.

Missions

Let's begin with simple definitions. In 1985, while reading *Commission* magazine at seminary, I was struck by the definitions of *mission* and *missions*:

> Mission is God's comprehensive, kingdom-related purpose to reconcile a lost world to himself. Missions is the activity or efforts of God's people to carry out the mission of God. Missions is the practical expression of God's mission.[3]

Missions is not a catchphrase or segmented program, but the obedient action of a church on mission. God expects his church to be *missional* in nature—to go forth and partner with him in his plans to reconcile the world. The word *missional* is a modern attempt to recapture the nature of the church. A *missional church* is really a *tautology* (two words that mean the same thing), even though for many it's become an oxymoron (or two words that mean the opposite). Mission and the church are inseparable. The problem is this is not reality for most of us.

The missional culture of an average church in North America does not resemble Acts in evangelistic impact, intentional disciple-making, influential shared-leadership, or community transformation. We are not seeing huge numbers of people come to Jesus or discipled in Christ. In fact, we often only see decline. This is because, over time, the original DNA of the church has mutated.

Do you remember playing the "telephone game" in school? The teacher would whisper a phrase or sentence to a student and then ask them to

---

[3] *The Commission* (Richmond, VA: International Mission Board, May 1996), 34.

whisper it to the next classmate. The message would travel to the last person, who would share with everyone what he or she had heard. The usual result was a distorted message. The more times a statement was passed along, the more distorted the message became. Genetic scientists say this is exactly what happens when DNA replication and transcription go awry.

These genetic mutations of missionary principles have ever increasingly crept into the church and, for the most part, are now accepted as normal values, behaviors, and beliefs (see appendix 6). Vance Havner states, "The church is so subnormal that if it ever got back to the New Testament normal it would seem to people to be abnormal."[4] Instead of our churches living missionally, now missions is often only done by proxy—writing a check or watching a missions video from a safe distance. A pastor recently shared with me in frustration, "Our church cannot even spell the word *missions*, let alone practice missions."

It doesn't have to be this way! The undeniable truth is the gospel and the kingdom of God break free and find a way—and Scripture shows us how. The solution for plateaued, hindered, and lifeless twenty-first-century churches is rediscovering and applying the spiritual DNA of the first-century church. Specifically, the book of Acts best illustrates how the gospel can penetrate every aspect of society and expand the influence of the church.

Like in physical DNA, in spiritual DNA there is a Holy Spirit-stirred, organic copying affect from the Source. Luke writes in Acts 1:1, "In the first book [the Gospel of Luke], O Theophilus, I have dealt with all that Jesus began to do and teach . . ." The order of these words is noteworthy because first Jesus "did" and then he "taught." He set a pattern. Jesus interpreted and evaluated the experiences of his disciples as they lived the missionary life. (This is also exactly what we will do in our journey through Acts: first we will do, then we will teach.) The first-century church only did what they saw Jesus doing. Author J. Vernon McGee wrote, "It is as if the four Gospels [have] been poured into a funnel, and they all come down into this jug of

---

[4] Vance Havner, *Pepper 'n Salt* (Grand Rapids: Revell, 1966), 9.

the first chapter of the Book of Acts."[5] Acts is a continuation of Jesus's life and ministry, and it's where we'll rediscover our original spiritual DNA.

Missionary Principles

As we journey together through the book of Acts, we will see how the early church grew and discover the ten missionary principles that make up the DNA structure of a church on mission. The ten principles and their corresponding church in Acts are:

1. Spiritual Preparation
   Wait, Pray, and Expect God to Work (Jerusalem)
2. Spiritual Authority
   Rely on the Holy Spirit's Power (Jerusalem)
3. Spiritual Understanding
   Focus on the Peoples and Places (Jerusalem/Caesarea)
4. Spiritual Leadership
   Identify and Nurture Missional Leaders (Antioch)
5. Spiritual Synergy
   Work Together for Greater Impact (Philippi)
6. Spiritual Receptivity
   Find the People of Peace (Philippi)
7. Spiritual Sowing
   Evangelize and Make Disciples (Thessalonica/Berea)
8. Spiritual Bridges
   Leverage Points of Connection (Athens)
9. Spiritual Giftedness
   Gather and Give Resources from the Harvest (Corinth)
10. Spiritual Warfare
    Fight the Good Fight (Ephesus)

---

[5] J. Vernon McGee, *Thru the Bible*, vol. 30, *Church History: Acts Chapters 1–14* (Nashville: Thomas Nelson, 1991), 2.

After each principle is a section titled "Acts Immersion." This section is designed to walk you or your small group through the principle and apply it to your life that week.

The first-century church faced many hindrances, such as complacency, persecution, prejudice, division, closed doors, seemingly limited resources, and cultural barriers. Sound familiar? Yet the church flourished in astounding ways, and so can we.

Before we begin our journey, let's talk about the two extremes we sometimes face in studying the book of Acts. I call this the Acts Spectrum (see graphic).

Figure 1
Acts Spectrum

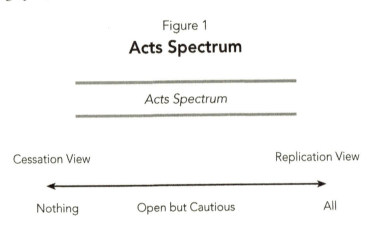

Adapted from the works of:
* Wayne A. Grudem, *Are Miraculous Gifts for Today?*, 142.
*Timothy Luke Johnson, *The Acts of the Apostles*, 3.

On one extreme are those who see the need to replicate everything they see in Acts in their modern environments—especially with a fixation on miracles, signs, and wonders. On the other end of the spectrum are those who believe that the supernatural ways of God in Acts were frozen in time, never to happen again (see *Are Miraculous Gifts for Today?* by Wayne Grudem for further study[6]). One extreme leads to abuse of the Word, the other to neglecting the Word. My personal understanding and conviction is that the answer lies somewhere in the middle. What we need to be careful of is any perspective hindering us from reading and hearing what God is speaking today from his Word—any extreme that would stop us from spreading the gospel.

As we together go on this missionary journey through Acts, it's noteworthy to revisit and consider the words of optimism about DNA from *Jurassic Park*:

> Biotechnology promises the greatest revolution in human history. By the end of this decade, it will have outdistanced atomic power and computers in its effect on our everyday lives. In the words of one observer, "Biotechnology is going to transform every aspect of human life: our medical care, our food, our health, our entertainment, and our very bodies. Nothing will ever be the same again. It's literally going to change the face of the planet."[7]

The church possesses something far more transformational than biotechnology: the hope of the gospel in Jesus Christ. It holds the promise for the greatest revolution in human history. It's the life of Christ breaking free and finding a way—a spontaneous expansion or movement of the gospel beyond human control. Listen to Roland Allen, late missionary from China, as he echoes this same thought:

> By spontaneous expansion I mean something which we cannot control. And if we cannot control it, we ought . . . to rejoice that we cannot control it. For if we cannot control it, it is because it is too great, not because it is too small for us. The great things of God are

---

[6] Wayne A. Grudem, *Are Miraculous Gifts for Today?: Four Views* (Grand Rapids: Zondervan, 1996), 23–89. The concept of the Acts Spectrum graphic is adapted from this work.

[7] Crichton, *Jurassic Park*, 83.

beyond our control. Therein lies a vast hope. Spontaneous expansion could fill the continents with the knowledge of Christ: our control cannot reach as far as that. We constantly bewail our limitations: open doors unentered; doors closed to us as foreign missionaries; fields white to harvest which we cannot reap. Spontaneous expansion could enter open doors, force closed ones, and reap those white fields. Our control cannot: it can only appeal pitifully for more men to maintain control.[8]

You have likely dreamed about being a part of a move of God like that. Now is the time!

---

[8] Roland Allen, *Spontaneous Expansion of the Church and the Causes That Hinder It* (Grand Rapids: Eerdmans, 1962), 13.

1

Spiritual Preparation: Wait, Pray, and Expect God to Work
(Jerusalem)

> *He [Jesus] also said to them, "This is what is written: The Messiah would suffer and rise from the dead the third day, and repentance for forgiveness of sins would be proclaimed in his name to all the nations, beginning at Jerusalem. You are witnesses of these things. And look I am sending you what my Father promised. As for you, stay in the city until you are empowered from on high."*
> —Luke 24:48–49

> *Expect great things from God; attempt great things for God.*
> —William Carey

"I like to wait!" . . . said no one ever. If there were a DNA gene for patient waiting, then William Carey would likely have possessed it. The shoemaker-turned-missionary, also known as the "Father of Modern Missions," spent years in faithful preparation. Early on, God used him to challenge a church in England paralyzed by hyper-Calvinism to rediscover their first-century spiritual DNA. From there he went on to India and, amazingly, <u>didn't see anyone come to Christ for seven years</u>. God did eventually give breakthroughs, the work did multipy, and others also answered the call to join him. Yet at his death, after <u>forty-one years in India</u>, <u>his converts numbered only in the hundreds</u>. We love the stories of thousands and tens of thousands coming to Christ. We love the stories of God invading our world and quickly doing what only he can do. But Scripture tells us of a critical step prior to any action. William Carey understood that the quiet work done in secret was as important as any great success in public.

Think for a moment about just how quickly and widely the gospel traveled in the book of Acts. Within only a few decades, much of the known world had heard the good news. The church in Jerusalem numbered 120 in an upper room, and exponentially grew in the city (some estimate 10,000 people), then moved from city to city, village to village, and continent to continent within a relatively short time.[1] That's a great deal of action happening in a great number of places. Now think about how it all began. Where did it start? With a command to wait.

At the end of Luke, Jesus instructs the church in Jerusalem to wait for the promise of the Father because they would be clothed and indwelt with the power of the Holy Spirit (24:49). The early disciples were people of action. Waiting was likely counterintuitive for them. However, <u>the book of Acts—the book of *action*—begins with waiting and preparation</u>. For the first-century church, the measure of the effectiveness on the mission field was directly related to the measure of spiritual preparation—praying, waiting, and expecting.

<u>The first strand of spiritual DNA in the church is to commit to</u> the Father's work of *spiritual preparation*. Jesus prepared the church at Jerusalem with forty days of instruction before his ascension, followed immediately by ten days of praying and waiting. When the Holy Spirit came upon them after that time of preparation, the church exploded with growth. Peter preached

---

[1] F. F. Bruce, "The Church of Jerusalem in the Acts of the Apostles," in *A Mind for What Matters: Collected Essays of F. F. Bruce* (Grand Rapids: Eerdmans, 1990), 151–52.

the gospel on the day of Pentecost and 3,000 received the gift of salvation through Christ. It's worth noting that the twenty-first century church tends to invert these priorities: it prays for minutes and then preaches for days, expecting Pentecost-like results.[2] If you and your church desire to see and experience an Acts 2 move of God, then you will need Acts 1 spiritual preparation.

There is always a direct connection between prayer and missions. Consider how prayer weaves through the account of the church start in Philippi:

- Paul and his companions went to the place of *prayer* with the gospel and met Lydia and the other women (Acts 16:13–14).
- They were on their way to *prayer* when they met the fortune-teller (16:16).
- Paul and Silas were *praying* and singing praise to God in prison chains when the Lord delivered them out of their chains and delivered a jailer and his household from their sin (16:25).

Preparation was *the* foundational missional principle for the church. It all began with a lifestyle of prayer, waiting, and expectation.

When a church takes the posture of wholeheartedly praying and waiting until the Lord says go—rather than relegating prayer to an event, program, or strategy—God does incredible things. To experience a move of God's Spirit and see lives transformed, we must not skip or shortcut the preliminary steps in the book of Acts.

God's Conditions to Revival

In the Bible, God sets forth conditions for revival. These conditions begin with spiritual preparation. It's important to note up front that we do not glibly say, "If we do x and y, then God will automatically do z," or assert

---

[2] Henry T. Blackaby and Avery T. Willis Jr., *On Mission with God: Living God's Purpose for His Glory* (Nashville: B&H, 2002), 177.

that God is obligated to respond to our prayers in a prescribed manner. God is sovereign and chooses to move with revival on his terms. However, his word does provide example after example of conditional promises related to revival and awakening. Billy Graham insightfully comments:

> As we have seen in this book [Acts], Pentecost was the day of power of the Holy Spirit. It was the day the Christian church was born. We do not expect that Pentecost will be repeated any more than that Jesus will die on the cross again. But we do expect Pentecostal blessings when the conditions for God's moving are met, and especially as we approach "the latter days." Christians are to prepare the way. We are to be ready for the Spirit to fill and use us.[3]

Consider 2 Chr 7:14. In the history of Israel, this verse was a call to spiritual preparation, and the life-changing actions are just as applicable to God's people today. The expectation and promise from God is: "If my people which are called by my name humble themselves, pray and seek my face, and turn from their wicked ways, then I will hear from heaven, forgive their sin and heal their land" (2 Chr 7:14 KJV). There is an "if" condition followed by a "then" outcome. Another conditional example is Moses's charge to God's people: "Now if you faithfully obey the LORD your God and are careful to follow all his commands I am giving you today, the LORD your God will put you far above all the nations of the earth" (Deut 28:1–2). The remainder of the chapter details the "then" blessings of obedience and the curses of disobedience. The prophet Joel gives us yet another conditional example when he called the nation to revival:

> Even now—this is the LORD's declaration—turn to me with all your heart, with fasting, weeping, and mourning. Tear your hearts, not just your clothes, and return to the LORD your God. For he is gracious and compassionate, slow to anger, abounding in faithful

---

[3] Billy Graham, *The Holy Spirit: Activating God's Power in Your Life* (Nashville: Thomas Nelson, 2011), 220.

love, and he relents from sending disaster. Who knows? He may turn and relent and leave a blessing behind him, so you can offer grain and wine to the LORD your God. (Joel 2:12–14)

This if-then pattern is repeated throughout Scripture.

Although Acts is not prescriptive in nature with "ifs" and "thens," it is a living description of what can happen when God's people pray, wait, and expect. If the early disciples would obediently wait for the Father's promise, then they would be baptized with the Holy Spirit (Acts 1:4–5). Jesus also instructed his disciples to ask the Lord of the harvest to send forth workers (Luke 10:32). Likewise, we should eagerly lean in to prayer as we wait and expect the Holy Spirit's power to permeate our lives, our churches, and our communities. In so doing, we can expect God to mobilize his people who are prepared and ready for the Holy Spirit's work.

The Purpose of Spiritual Preparation

God's principle lessons during times of waiting are trust, obedience, and character building. The Jerusalem church's experience points to this truth. Stephen, one of the first deacons, preached a powerful sermon in Jerusalem about the redemptive history of God's people, giving us a glimpse of these lessons. Look at how God uses seasons of preparation in his mission:

- Stephen starts with Abraham and how God worked in his life (Acts 7:1–8). Abraham waited twenty-five years to see God's promise fulfilled (Gen 12:4; 21:4). He was told God's people would wait for 400 years to be set free from bondage (Acts 7:6–7). God taught him to trust and obey (Rom 4:16–25).
- He mentions Joseph in Egypt (Acts 7:9–16). Joseph waited thirteen years while God built his character and a heart to forgive (Gen 37:2; 41:46). God sent him ahead to prepare the way (Ps 105:17–22).
- He turns to Moses (Acts 7:17–50). God shaped Moses's character to match the assignment. That work took forty years in the desert and forty more years wandering in the wilderness (Acts 7:30, 36).

Seasons of preparation hold serious purpose. God is not delaying action but rather making us ready to carry his agenda. God expects trust, obedience, and character from his servants on mission with him. It's in his waiting rooms (or upper rooms) where he prepares his people. The Jerusalem church would be no different.

Spiritual Preparation Leads to Specific Direction

In addition to the work it does in our hearts to build our faith, spiritual preparation also provides specific direction to our steps. Jesus spent extended time in intense personal prayer. He often retreated from the crowds in order to seek the Father. It may sound like an odd question, but have you ever considered what Jesus prayed about? Could it be that Jesus was asking God to reveal his next steps to him? What town do I go to next? Who do I talk to? Jesus received direction and strength as he waited on the Father for his next steps.

Friends, this is our example. How do we know what city or neighborhood to plant a church in? How do we know what our role is to be in a missionary endeavor or what new ministry our city needs? How will we be able to discern when God is bringing someone into our lives to share the gospel? The church in Jerusalem had a clear command from Jesus to wait for the promise of the Father. If we follow his lead, we will experience his power and presence.

Each word from God will be unique to your context and always in alignment with his Word. God may direct you to start a new ministry inspired by a need in your community like for the widows in Acts 6. God may send a confirming word to you as you select a missional leader or church planter, like he did for the Antioch missionary team in Acts 13. God may send you to a specific place or people group to engage like Macedonia in Acts 16. Acts implies action, but waiting on the Lord's direction was and still is God's first step in accomplishing his mission.

Spiritual Preparation Leads to a Kingdom Focus

Time spent in prayer and expectant waiting also aligns our focus to God's focus. The book of Acts begins with the kingdom of God (1:3) and ends with the kingdom of God (28:31). Jesus was only about the kingdom of God: "The Son of Man has come *to seek and to save that which was lost*" and "The kingdom of God is not coming with something observable; no one will say, 'See here!' or 'There!' For you see, *the kingdom of God is in your midst.*" (Luke 17:21; 19:1–10, emphasis added). But despite all that Jesus said and taught about his kingdom during his ministry, the infant church in Jerusalem was still more concerned about restoring the political kingdom to Israel—a purely earthly mindset missing the point of the redemption of lost souls. God needed to readjust their earthly thinking to a kingdom focus: to the reign and rule of Jesus Christ in a person's heart. Kingdom advance occurs through making disciples who make disciples as the gospel flows from person to person. God's kingdom is our priority and should be tenaciously guarded.

The First Great Awakening, from 1734 to 1770, was marked by spiritual preparation. When God chose to move in America, he used Jonathan Edwards's preaching (among others) to bring great revival to the colonies. Edwards understood the significance of spiritual preparation when he called for an "explicit agreement and visible union of the people of God in extraordinary prayer for revival of religion and the advancement of Christ's kingdom on earth."[4] Notice the kingdom focus. It wasn't Edwards's kingdom; it wasn't a certain church's kingdom. Edwards helped call the early American colonies back to a vibrant, personal faith that grew

---

[4] Jonathan Edwards, *An Humble Attempt to Promote Explicit Agreement and Visible Union of God's People in Extraordinary Prayer, for the Revival of Religion and the Advancement of Christ's Kingdom on Earth*, in *The Complete Works of Jonathan Edwards*, ed. Sereno Dwight, repr. (Edinburgh: Banner of Truth Trust, 1986), 294.

like wildfire from neighbor to neighbor, disciple to disciple. His kingdom focus was undeterred.

Think of the church like a focused parachute packer. The pastor and the church are entrusted with souls just as the parachute packer is responsible for the skydiver's life. A failed chute in the natural means certain death like a distorted or uneven focus in the spiritual can be catastrophic. If you were the skydiver, would you want your parachute packer distracted by other priorities? What if he got a call and hurried out before including the emergency chute? As everyday Christ followers and leaders in the church, we are called to help people prepare for eternity with Jesus. This requires clear, constant, steady focus on the mission. Ask the Lord to show you areas of misplaced focus and distractions that draw you away from the mission. Ask for a hunger to make disciples in your context. Address those areas with a renewed focus and singular mind-set of God's kingdom and not your own.

Spiritual Preparation Leads to Unity

Any powerful move of God can be traced to an individual or a group that sought God in a season of concentrated, unified, and fervent prayer. J. Edwin Orr, quoting A. T. Pierson in a message about awakenings said, "There has never been a spiritual awakening in any country or locality that did not begin in united prayer."[5] The first church in Jerusalem was no exception. They were united in prayer first and then experienced a spiritual awakening.

Prayer magnetically pulls God's people together. The shared mission pulls God's people together. God's love pulls his people together. Jesus fervently prayed:

---

[5] J. Edwin Orr, "Prayer and Revival," from a lecture at a Prayer Congress in Dallas, available online at http://www.jedwinorr.com/resources/articles/prayandrevival.pdf, accessed May 30, 2019.

I pray not only for these, but also for those who believe in me through their word. May they all be one, as you, Father, are in me and I am in you. May they also be in us, so that the world may believe you sent me. I have given them the glory you have given me, so that they may be one as we are one. I am in them and you are in me, so that they may be made completely one, that the world may know you have sent me and have loved them as you have loved me. (John 17:20–23)

His prayers never go unanswered. You and I are the specific answer to that high priestly prayer of Jesus. Unified in love. Unified in purpose. Unified in witness to a lost world. This is what happens when we stop and pray.

A Twenty-First-Century Example—Spiritual Preparation Expressed

The Church of the Beloved, located in Chicago, Illinois, is a great example of a church birthed and sustained in prayer. Because of practicing the principle of spiritual preparation, it is seeing God move in powerful ways. Former pastor David Choi didn't intend to start a church there. He went to the Billy Graham Museum at Wheaton College to pray about an offer to pastor a church in California. But instead, in that time of prayer, he heard the Lord's call to plant a church in Chicago. God spoke to him through Exod 33:11–23 and he knew that God's presence would go with him as with Moses. He said, "I felt God tell me, 'I'm going to lead you to a place to plant. You're not going to be alone because I'm going to be with you. Is my presence enough?'"[6] Choi's response was "Yes!" The promise of God's presence is exactly what each of us needs when on God's mission.

Choi enthusiastically shared that a prayer-filled church is a Spirit-filled church, but a prayerless church is Spirit-less church. One of the

---

[6] Tobin Perry, "Choi Takes Multicultural Aim in Windy City," Baptist Press, July 29, 2013, http://www.bpnews.net/40811/choi-takes-multicultural-aim-in-windy-city.

Church of the Beloved's core values is "dependent prayer." It is woven into the fabric of their fellowship. United in one accord, they pray for an hour before every service. They have two hour-long scheduled prayer meetings every month, and every year the church has a twenty-one-day Daniel fast to pray, wait, and expect God to move among them. Choi said, "Because of that, by God's mercy, in four years there have been four churches planted in three different cities, with more than 700 people attending, reaching thirty-five nations, and with more than 100 people coming to Christ just this past year." When believers are in one accord, they are centered on the person of Jesus Christ and his mission purposes. Augustine was credited with the statement, "In essentials, unity; in doubtful matters, liberty; in all things, charity."[7] People in the church can disagree about many things but the essential gospel mission of Jesus is not ambiguous. Where love abounds so will mission action. We must decide to do everything possible to work toward and maintain missional unity within the church.

Conclusion

Jesus knew and modeled the importance of spiritual preparation. The church he planted in Jerusalem followed their teacher's lead (see appendix 3), praying and waiting expectantly for God to work. Henry Blackaby and Avery Willis ask the question: "If God told the people in your church to stop everything and spend ten days in prayer for revival, how would they respond?"[8] How would you and I respond?

Author and speaker Terry Teykel coined the phrase "pray the price."[9] Are you and I willing to count the cost for spiritual awakening and revival?

---

[7] This quote is widely attributed to Augustine of Hippo, although this is contested by many, with various other theories of origin.

[8] Blackaby and Willis, *On Mission with God*, 176.

[9] Terry Teykel, *Pray the Price*, ed. Lynn Ponder (Muncie, IN: Prayer Point Press, 1997), 2.

Are we willing to invest ourselves in God's kingdom first, setting aside our own comfort and agenda? Are we willing to come together in unity? When we make the decision to meet God's conditions, the Holy Spirit responds and dynamically infuses you and I with his spiritual DNA to continue the mission of Jesus on earth.

Acts Immersion

Acts Action Item

Commit to the Father's work of spiritual preparation in your life and the life of your church.

Culture Change: Basic Training and Preparation

Each branch of the military begins with basic training. It's an immersive experience to infuse new recruits with the DNA of their new life. It helps to develop a unified team and creates a culture of excellence among recruits. The soldier's ability to survive and thrive is inexplicably linked to basic training. The *US Army Leadership Field Manual* reads:

> You have been entrusted with a great responsibility. How do you prepare yourself? How do you learn and embrace those values and skills that will enable you to meet the challenge?
>
> This manual is a tool to help you answer these questions, to begin or continue becoming a leader of character and competence, an Army leader. . . . [w]hat you must BE, KNOW, and DO as an Army leader.[10]

Notice the order here: be, know, then do. Everything flows from who we are first, our training second, and our action third. Basic training prepares a soldier for battle and the missions ahead. Spiritual preparation is the beginning of basic training for the missional life.

---

[10] The Center for Army Leadership *US Army Leadership Field Manual* (New York: McGraw-Hill, 2004), 2.

Acts Character and Competence

Be...

- prayerful—waiting on the Holy Spirit's power to witness
- united—to one another in love and missionary purpose
- expectant—to be empowered by the Holy Spirit to live like a missionary

Know...

- that Jesus was the first Church Planter establishing the church in Jerusalem
- that the kingdom work of evangelism, disciple making, and church planting requires spiritual preparation
- that constant, unified prayer was at the heart of the preparation

Do...

- Prayerfully read the daily devotional "Acts Moment"* and the Acts Bible readings below.
- Clear up any relationships that are not right by seeking restoration and unity.
- Ask God to show you points of kingdom refocus in your life and mission.
- Engage in a prayer walk or drive this week—praying on site with insight.
- Ask God to fill you with his Holy Spirit afresh and anew to be his witness.
- Commit to utilize the *ACTS Prayer Guide* at the weekly corporate prayer or your personal prayer time.*

Acts Readings

Day 1: Acts 1:1–11
Day 2: Acts 1:12–26
Day 3: Acts 2:1–13
Day 4: Acts 2:14–41
Day 5: Acts 2:42–47

Acts Missionary Activity

Prayer Walking and Visits

This week team up with someone for a prayer walk and engage the residents of at least two homes. Knock on the door, and when they answer, say, "Hello, My name is _____. We [or our church] have committed to praying for the families in this neighborhood." Then ask, "How can we pray for you today . . . family, financial, health, or other concerns?" After they express their needs, ask if you could pray for them right then. Pray for their request(s) and pray the gospel (thanking God for the good news of Jesus dying on the cross for our sins and rising from the dead to give us forgiveness and a new life). Thank them for allowing you to pray with them and begin to look for ways to follow up with them. For example, you could invite them to a Bible study or church event. You might ask them the open-ended question, what can I do for you? Then take specific actions to meet that need in a timely manner.

Reflection: With prayer as the focus, how did you see God preparing the way for your visit?

Spiritual Preparation in the Life of Christ

Jesus modeled the spiritual DNA of praying and expectantly waiting on the Father to work through specific direction, kingdom focus, and unity.

For Further Reading

- *Experiencing God* by Henry Blackaby and Claude King
- *Spiritual Disciplines* by Don Whitney
- *Pray the Price* by Terry Terkel

*There are two options available for you to obtain the *Acts Bible Readings Guides, Acts Moments Daily Devotional, Acts Small Group Guides, Acts Missionary Experiences* and *ACTS Prayer Guides*. First, these are all conveniently located in the "Participants Hub" of the supplemental resource *The Spiritual DNA of a Church on Mission Workbook*. Secondly, you will be able to easily download these along with other helpful Spiritual DNA resources for you and your church to use on the website www.bobburton.net. These may be used either individually, within small groups, or during your own church-wide season of missional revival.

2

Spiritual Authority: Rely on the Holy Spirit's Power
(Jerusalem)

Jesus came near and said to them, "All authority has been given to me in heaven and on earth."
—Matthew 28:18

We are guilty of forgetting the authority of the Holy Spirit. We are so interested in ourselves and in our own activities that we have forgotten the one thing that can make us effective.
—D. M. Lloyd-Jones, "The Authority of the Holy Spirit"

DNA functions a lot like an office copy machine. It has the incredible ability to replicate itself perfectly. The purpose of DNA replication is to produce two identical copies of a DNA molecule—which is critical when cells are dividing and forming new cells. If DNA does not duplicate exactly, one of the new cells could receive all the DNA information and the other cell could receive none, or each cell could receive only part of the DNA.

Either way, life could not continue as it was. This precise copying effect is nothing short of the stuff of life.[1]

The Holy Spirit works in similar fashion to a copy machine, replicating the work of Christ in and through us. We are each of us to become, as C. S. Lewis said, a "little Christ," following Christ's missional example in words and actions.[2] This is only possible through complete reliance on the Holy Spirit. As a Christ follower, the influence of Jesus's holy life will impart a powerful copying affect translated into obedient, kingdom-first living. The second strand of spiritual DNA is *spiritual authority*. If we are to become "little Christs," then we must surrender to and operate out of spiritual authority as he did. Spiritual authority is receiving and relying on the Holy Spirit in every part of your life and ministry.

Spiritual Authority in the Life of Christ

Think about the story of the centurion who asked Jesus to heal his servant (Matt 8:5–13). Jesus was impressed with his faith and understanding of spiritual authority. He said to Jesus, "For I am too a man under authority, with soldiers underneath me. And I say to one 'Go' and he goes, and to another, 'Come' and he comes, to my servant, 'Do this' and he does it" (v. 9). The Lord was pleased with his attitude and understanding of authority. He believed the Lord was in charge, had the power to heal with just a word, and could be everywhere just like the Holy Spirit. Jesus called it for what it was: an act and statement of faith. Jesus's authority must still be unquestionably followed. It is the essence of the Lordship of Christ.

A reiteration of the Great Commission is in the Gospels four times and one time in Acts. Starting in Acts, Jesus said to them, "It is not for you to know times or periods that the Father has set by his own authority. But you will receive power when the Holy Spirit has come on you, and

---

[1] Tara Rodden Robinson, *Genetics for Dummies*, 2nd ed. (Hoboken, NJ: John Wiley and Sons, 2010), 99.

[2] C. S. Lewis, *Mere Christianity* (New York: Touchstone 1996), 153–54.

you will be my witnesses in Jerusalem, in all Judea and Samaria, and to the end of the earth" (Acts 1:7–8). This missional command is in the context of the Father's authority and the power of the Holy Spirit. Another command in Matt 28:18–20 focuses on his authority and the promise of his presence—the Holy Spirit. "Jesus came near and said to them, 'All authority has been given to me in heaven and on earth'" (v. 18) and then sandwiched in between the missional actions . . . he says, "And remember, I am with you always, to the end of the age" (v. 20b). These missionary announcements speak to the command to be on mission with him.

Spiritual authority extended to Jesus's followers as well. He taught and spoke often of the Holy Spirit's coming to baptize, indwell, empower, convict, and comfort his followers. The risen Jesus commissioned his disciples by breathing on them the Holy Spirit and saying, "As the Father has sent me, even so have I sent you" (John 20:21).

- "He gave them authority over unclean spirits, to drive them out and to heal every disease and sickness." (Matt 10:1)
- "He appointed seventy-two others, and he sent them ahead of him in pairs to every town and place where he himself was about to go." (Luke 10:1)
- "He summoned the Twelve and began to send them out in pairs and gave them authority over unclean spirits." (Mark 6:7)

The disciples went forth receiving and relying on the Holy Spirit. In his book *The DNA of a Revolution*, Gary Mayes writes, "When God entrusted us with his mission in the world, he wired us for dependency on him. In that posture of dependency, we discover true spiritual authority."[3] Our everyday walk as Christians is not to be powered by our own ambition or driven by our personal plans or best strategies. The principle of spiritual authority is that we mirror Jesus's example, relying on the Holy Spirit in every way.

---

[3] Gary Mayes, *DNA of a Revolution: 1st Century Breakthroughs That Will Transform the Church* (Charleston, SC: Long Wake, 2013), 189.

This reliance includes our personal walk and also extends to missions. In the discourse to the twelve disciples, Jesus said the Holy Spirit would give them the words to say while serving on mission (Matt 10:19–20). In Acts, we see the church relying heavily on the Holy Spirit—before councils of men, while combating the enemy, and while bringing healing to those in need. Jeff Christopherson with the Send Network says, "What made the first century church so potent was its absolute disinterest in itself. It saw its reason to be as a catalyst for the Kingdom, emulating the pattern lived out by its founders (who followed the standard set by the Founder). Kingdom first."[4] The new church in Jerusalem was marked by a *complete reliance* on the Holy Spirit's power for boldly sharing the gospel message and for the expansion of God's kingdom. Let's take a closer look at the early church in Acts to explore what practicing the DNA principle of spiritual authority looked like in their world and what it continues to look like in ours.

How the Early Church Relied on the Holy Spirit

In every western movie is invariably a scene in which a sheriff forms a posse to go after the bad guys. He deputizes and sends these volunteers with the full authority of the law to back them up. In a sense, Jesus deputized and sent out his followers to make disciples of all peoples. The book of Acts gives us the best practices for what deputized Christ followers need in order to operate within their God-given spiritual authority. Keep in mind these can only be put into practice and sustained by relying wholly on the Holy Spirit.

Spiritually Authorized People Imitate Jesus

In order to operate with spiritual authority, the early church walked and talked like Jesus did. In fact, the followers of Jesus were first called "Christians" or "little Christs" in Antioch (Acts 11:26). The term was initially intended by

---

[4] Jeff Christopherson and Mac Lake, *Kingdom First: Starting Churches That Shape Movements* (Nashville: B&H, 2015), 6.

outsiders as derisive, but Christians won over the outsiders because of how they lived their lives. Commentator Kenneth Wuest makes the case that each of the three times the New Testament uses the word *Christians*, it was derogatory. Wuest states that the city of Antioch had a reputation for coming up with such nicknames.[5] By their Spirit-directed actions those "little Christs" were given a necessary platform to boldly proclaim the gospel.

It is totally impossible to live like Jesus and obey his Great Commission without the power of the Holy Spirit. Far too often there is little that distinguishes a professing believer from the non-believing world. Our spiritual authority is nullified if our talk and walk are empty. The spiritual authority experienced by the early church flowed first out of relationship with Jesus and then out of ever-growing relationship with the Spirit. Consider that Jesus first called his disciples to be *with* him and that even his teachings were rooted in loving relationship with his disciples. It was first and foremost about relationship—and that is still the essence of discipleship today (Mark 3:14). The Spirit of Christ within us is the teacher. As we grow in relationship with him, he will empower us to walk and talk as Jesus did.

Spiritually Authorized People Obey Orders

To operate in spiritual authority, the believers in Acts obeyed orders. These earliest followers had trouble understanding just exactly what God's kingdom was. They asked, "Lord, are you restoring the kingdom to Israel at this time?" (Acts 1:6). Jesus replied that it wasn't theirs to know. They had missed the point again. Their business was not to be about earthly rule but to be about Jesus's orders—"But you will receive power when the Holy Spirit has come on you, and you will be my witnesses in Jerusalem, in all Judea and Samaria, and to the end of the earth" (Acts 1:8). Jesus in effect said: "Obey God, and live in the dynamic power of the Holy Spirit! God has commanded you to make disciples and announced that you will be his

---

[5] Kenneth Samuel Wuest, *Wuest's Word Studies of the Greek New Testament* (Grand Rapids: Eerdmans, 1973), 1:19.

witnesses here, there, and everywhere." How did these believers respond? They obeyed even when they didn't fully understand.

Jesus's command and promise were and are the authoritative mission of the kingdom. Our role continues to be to obey him. At times we get distracted by politics, our own ambitions, hurt feelings, confusion, or fear, but the priority of the kingdom is an obedience issue for us just like it was for the earliest followers. We are to obey our orders even when we don't understand God's purposes behind them (which, if we're honest, is much of the time). Whether the Spirit's orders are about our focus, the details of our day, or witnessing to our neighbor, obedience to the King in every matter is key to operating in spiritual authority.

Spiritually Authorized People Witness for Christ

We operate with spiritual authority when we witness in the Spirit's power. In the first chapter of Acts the early followers waited for the promise of the Father based on instructions from Jesus. Jesus said, "you will be baptized with the Holy Spirit not many days from now" (Acts 1:5) so that "you will be my witnesses" (Acts 1:8). The instructions for the early church and for us are twofold: be filled with the Spirit and witness boldly for Christ.

It's important to note there are two parts to the filling of the Spirit. First, every believer is baptized by the Spirit at the point of their new birth. The apostle Paul affirmed, "For we were all baptized by one Spirit into one body—whether Jews, Greeks, whether slaves or free—and we were all given one Spirit to drink" (1 Cor 12:13). This immersion of the Spirit automatically occurs at the point of each person's salvation.

The second part to the filling of the Spirit is an ongoing experience based on our growing relationship with the Lord Jesus. This distinction is important because it underlies the need for consistent refilling for all believers (Eph 5:18). Without it, our personal walk and our missional progress suffer. Because of the battle with our sin nature, Christians are leaky vessels needing the filling of God's Spirit over and over again. Make no mistake:

even though Christians leak, God has promised to seal, keep, and guard his children by the Holy Spirit unto salvation (2 Cor 1:22; Eph 1:13; Phil 1:6; 1 Pet 1:3–5). He will never leave nor forsake or run out; the truth is even embedded in Jesus's missionary mandate for the church (Matt 28:19–20). He promised to be with us always, and that is through his Spirit inside you.

What does it look like to be initially and continually filled with the Spirit?

- A life of missionary action for Christ (witness by the Spirit),
- A life of character traits like Christ (fruit of the Spirit),
- A life of spiritual giftedness from Christ (gifts of the Spirit).

Isn't it interesting that the most often overlooked marker of a Spirit-filled believer is missionary action? Commentator Ajith Fernando writes, "His last command should be our first concern."[6] The Holy Spirit did not come to attract attention to himself but, as Joel prophesied, he came upon those first-century believers (young and old, male and female) to empower them to witness for Christ and extend an open invitation to call upon the Lord for salvation (Joel 2:28–32; Acts 2:16–21). The missionary Henry Martyn said, "The Spirit of Christ is the spirit of missions. The nearer we get to Him, the more intensely missionary we become."[7] Sharing the gospel is not optional for us. It is part of our very DNA!

Spiritual Authorized People Are Accountable

Operating out of spiritual authority also looks like accountability. The first church assembled in the Upper Room collectively made decisions and practiced spiritual authority through a Spirit-appointed leadership structure.

---

[6] Ajith Fernando, *The NIV Application Commentary: Acts* (Grand Rapids: Zondervan, 2015), 57.

[7] The Board of Missions of the Protestant Episcopal Church, *The Spirit of Missions* (New York: J. L. Powell, 1892), 57:90, 134.

Throughout Acts, there was a wide array of Spirit-appointed leaders who provided missional accountability and service to one another. This accountability was not only for leaders but extended to Christ followers who first met from house to house for prayer, teaching, sharing resources, the breaking of bread, and worshiping God together (Acts 4:42–47). Each church in Acts was autonomous and self-governing with their own structures of authority while at the same time cooperating in relationship with other churches for a voluntary mutual accountability.

This Spirit-reliant church in Jerusalem maintained unity by protecting their moral and doctrinal purity for the sake of Christ's mission.

- Peter confronted Ananias and Sappharia in their deception (Acts 5:1–11). This couple's grievous sins were directly against the person of the Holy Spirit (vv. 3, 9).
- The church had to contend with complaints regarding the neglect of the Grecian widows' daily care. The proposed solution became an occasion for the church to exercise mutual accountability for missional advance. Responsible men, the first deacons, were selected based on the following qualities: Holy-Spirit filled, good reputation, and wisdom (Acts 6:1–7). The result was immediate kingdom multiplication.
- At the Jerusalem Council, God's people gathered together to make decisions and hold one another accountable on the nature of the gospel. Spiritual authority unified the church around the affirmation that the gospel is defined in Christ's redemptive work alone without adding the rite of circumcision (Acts 15).
- Philip dealt firmly with Simon the sorcerer, who attempted to buy the Holy Spirit like a cheap commodity. Then led by the Spirit, Philip met with the Ethiopian eunuch who was sitting in his chariot, trying to understand Isaiah. He preached the gospel with full reliance on the Holy Spirit and the Scriptures. He then baptized the Ethiopian with the authority of the church (Acts 8:9–25).

God used these first-century men on mission, and many others like them, to keep brothers and sisters focused on Christ's mission above all else.

Accountability among brothers and sisters is equally as important today as it was in the early church. It's been said that we are all just one step from stupid. With that in mind, spiritual leaders and church members must take a militant stand on protecting fellow brothers and sisters in Christ. Seek out accountability. Set the example. Have the courage to lovingly confront someone pressing the boundaries and playing with fire. Be strong as a soldier of Christ, not leaving anyone behind, and be willing to restore another if they have given in to temptation (Gal 6:1; 2 Tim 2:1).

A Twenty-First Century Example—Spiritual Authority Expressed

Pastor Clint Clifton heeded God's call to plant Pillar Church near the Marine Corps base in Quantico, Virginia—the crossroads and hub of the Marine Corps (USMC)—to reach those serving in the military and their families. God gave the church a vision not just for one city but to reach people for Christ and plant a church near each of the four major clusters of Marine Corps bases in the world. There is a multiplication factor built into this God-given strategy for reaching the military, very much like the Roman soldiers in Acts. The very DNA of a Marine is one of a rapid deployable mobile force by land, sea, or air, and in like manner they and their families are frequently reassigned to new bases. Pillar Church wants to be their church family no matter where they are assigned.

Pastor Clint has learned a lot about spiritual authority during his tenure at Pillar Church. He says, "The task God called us to seemed so big and impossible that I viewed the power of the Holy Spirit to be our only hope for accomplishing the goals set before us. The magnitude of the task pushed me into a deep reliance on the Spirit's power for our progress." He goes on to say, "A mentor advised me in [the early] days to put myself in Peter's position out on the water, drowning unless Christ held me up. Now, when I look back at all that has been accomplished and all that God is doing I know that the Holy Spirit has been at work. I know I had very little to do with it, and I know that if we are to do anything significant in the future, it will be the continuation of the work of the Spirit."[8] This is the essence of spiritual authority at work in our lives: utter dependence on the Spirit and total obedience to God's call.

Conclusion

Both the centurion who interacted with Jesus as well as my church planter friend have demonstrated impressive examples of what it is to walk in the authority and influence of the Holy Spirit. The Jerusalem church received the infilling of the Holy Spirit for the purpose of living on mission for Christ. It's providential that military personnel throughout the New Testament were receptive because they truly understand authority and the concept of mission. Consequently, a good number of those early believers came from the Roman army and their mobility helped to spread the gospel.

Reflect for a moment on the principle of spiritual authority in your life. Is the Lord pleased with your understanding and personal application of spiritual authority? If God asked you today to plant a church like Pastor Clint or turn down a lucrative job, volunteer in your children's school or knock on your neighbor's door to share the gospel with them, how would you respond? Would you talk and walk like Jesus? Would you obey his instructions no matter how uncomfortable, inconvenient, or contrary to your plans? Would you witness boldly in the Spirit's power? Would you hold yourself and your brothers and sisters accountable to upright living?

The same Holy Spirit dynamically alive in those first-century believers is dynamically alive in twenty-first century believers. The same Spirit who rose Jesus from the dead lives in us as born-again believers (Rom 8:9–11). He is the resurrection power living on the inside. The Greek word translated

---

[8] Clint Clifton, North American Mission Board Send City Missionary, email message to the author, January 28, 2017. For more on Pillar Church, see http://pillarchurchsbc.com/.

power in Acts 1:8 is the origin for the modern English word "dynamite." Think of a megaton atomic explosion and multiply that trillions of times over, and you are still not even close to the awesome power of God's Spirit. The most important question is not do you have the Holy Spirit, but does the Holy Spirit completely have you?[9]

---

[9] Michael Green, *Thirty Years That Changed the World: The Book of Acts for Today* (Grand Rapids: Eerdmans, 2002), 6.

Acts Immersion

Acts Action Item

Continuously receive and rely on the Holy Spirit, the Father's promise of spiritual authority in your life and the life of your church.

Culture Change: DNA Test for a Church and Accountablity

What if it were possible to have your church take a spiritual DNA test? The challenge for any church is to measure up to the church in Acts. A church expressing the DNA of spiritual authority is not fixated on exalting the Holy Spirit but Jesus Christ. Theologian J. I. Packer states, "The Spirit's message to us is never, 'Look at me; listen to me; come to me; get to know me,' but always, 'Look at him, and see his glory; listen to him, and hear his word; go to him, and have life; get to know him, and taste his gift of joy and peace.'"[10] The Holy Spirit always makes much of Jesus and making much of Jesus will, in turn, lead to making much of his mission. If your church took a DNA test, would it reveal a community of believers continually receiving and relying on the Holy Spirit? Would every area of the church point to Jesus and make much of him? This is the defining mark of a Holy Spirit-reliant church in the truest sense of the word.

Acts Character and Competence

Be . . .

- Spirit-filled witnesses—share Christ in the power of the Holy Spirit
- submissive—to the Holy Spirit's call to engage the lost with spiritual authority

---

[10] J. I. Packer, *Keep in Step with the Spirit: Finding Fullness in Our Walk with God* (Grand Rapids: Baker Book House, 2005), 57.

- empowered—by receiving and relying on the Holy Spirit as you seek his kingdom first

Know...

- that Acts 1:8 is an announcement of the Holy Spirit's power and presence for witness
- that true spiritual authority comes through reliance on the Holy Spirit
- that we imitate Jesus Christ through the power of the Holy Spirit
- that believers hold each other accountable through the Holy Spirit

Do...

- Prayerfully read the daily devotional "Acts Moment" and the Acts Bible readings below.
- Exercise your spiritual authority in Christ to witness to someone God brings your way this week.
- Ask God to fill you with his Holy Spirit afresh and anew to be his witness.
- Commit to utilize the *ACTS Prayer Guide* at the weekly corporate prayer or your personal prayer time.

Acts Readings

Day 1: Acts 3:1–10
Day 2: Acts 3:11–26
Day 3: Acts 4:1–22
Day 4: Acts 4:23–31
Day 5: Acts 4:32–37

Acts Missionary Activity

Sharing Jesus with Spiritual Authority

This week, ask the Lord for a divine appointment to share Christ with someone. Remembering all the spiritual authority vested in you by God, ask the person about their eternal destiny. Use your own words and do so with love. Share your testimony. Be prepared for that person to respond and be ready to present the gospel. Leave the results to the Holy Spirit as you share Jesus. You could start by simply asking, "How far are you from God?" or "How close are you to God?" Or you might ask, "If God could do a miracle in your life, what would you want him to do?" After they share, ask, "Can I share a miracle in my life?" Then share your testimony. Be a good listener and rest on the promise that the Holy Spirit will give you the right words (Matt 10:19–20).

Reflection: Knowing that you have spiritual authority, how did it make a difference in your confidence to share Jesus?

Spiritual Authority in the Life of Christ

Jesus modeled spiritual authority through relying on the Holy Spirit in every domain of his life.

For Further Reading

- *The Holy Spirit* by Billy Graham
- *The Spirit, the Church and the World* by John Stott
- *Jesus Continued* by J. D. Greear

3

Spiritual Understanding: Focus on Peoples and Places
(Jerusalem and Caesarea)

From one man, he has made every nationality to live over the whole earth and has determined their appointed times and the boundaries of where they live. He did this so that they might seek God, and perhaps they might reach out and find him, though he is not far from each one of us.
—Acts 17:26–27

We need to learn the heart language of the people and to share the gospel with them in their language.
—Ajith Fernando, *The NIV Application Commentary: Acts*

DNA testing revolutionized what we can learn about ourselves and our personal genealogies. The DNA "spit test" to discover a person's heritage, sometimes followed by a trip to the newly discovered motherland, has led many people to a greater exploration and understanding of their personal identity and the places of their ancestral roots. Much like this personal quest to learn more of our genealogical heritage, the DNA of spiritual understanding is the way God focuses our attention on specific people and places to share the gospel. Similarly to discovering surprising results of a physical DNA test, sometimes the people and places God highlights to us for evangelism are ones we've never seen before—and they're right in our own backyards.

Caesarea Movement—the DNA of Reaching the Gentiles

The most striking example of the principle of spiritual understanding is found in Acts 10: the story of Peter, a Jew, sharing the good news with Cornelius, a Gentile. Peter, like all the apostles, went from town to town sharing the good news of Jesus largely with other Jews. The earliest "Christians" were Jews and these early followers didn't initially understand that the gospel was intended for others as well. Through a vision, God corrects Peter's thinking and instructs him the gospel is for all nations, Jew and Gentile alike (Gal 3:27–29). God confronted Peter's own ethnic prejudice and then orchestrated a meeting with Cornelius, a God-fearing Gentile.

Peter obediently preached the gospel in Cornelius's home and, in another Pentecost-type event, Cornelius's entire household came to faith: "While Peter was still speaking these words, the Holy Spirit came down on all those who heard the message" (Acts 10:44). Just like those at Pentecost, those present in Cornelius's home spoke in other languages, declaring the greatness of God to one another.

The first-century church crossed incredible barriers of race and culture and the same need exists for us today. Spiritual understanding begins when we recognize the gospel is for all. It's not just for the Jews; it's for every nation. It's not just a message for us in our comfortable church pews; it's for everyone in our city and the world. God is still at work changing our hearts and beliefs to open our eyes to different peoples and places around us.

Let's pause a moment to consider how Luke shares this story in Acts 10. He first describes Cornelius: his location is Caesarea, his language group is likely Italian, and his affinity group is military (Acts 10:1). These three descriptions are incredibly insightful. Van Sanders, a missiologist, proposes that people groups can be placed on a spectrum based on preferences to three areas: location, language, or affinity.[1] Each person has a preferred heart language—a natural bent—toward their location, their language, or their affinity group. Understanding a person's preferred heart language and its unique distinctives guides us to the best methodology and setting to reach the person for Christ. For example, much like Pillar Church's strategy to reach the USMC, a soldier's preferred heart language is often his or her military affinity group. The missionary method is not a one-size-fits-all strategy but ought to be customized for each individual and people group.

Historically, when we've talked about sharing our faith with others, we often think only of one segment of people. This is unfortunate because it's quite limiting. Missiologist David Garrison defines a *people group* as "The largest group through which the gospel can flow without encountering significant barriers of understanding and acceptance."[2] Most of us see our mission fields consisting of folks just like us but our communities are usually surprisingly diverse: already hosting many different language groups and an incredible variety of affinity-based networks. There can also be locations within our communities in great need of the gospel. This new way of thinking and seeing can be a game changer. Missiologists like Ralph Winter describe these kinds of peoples as "hidden in plain sight."[3] Let's truly see the people and explore specific ways spiritual understanding can highlight people groups and places the Lord is calling us to.

---

[1] Van Sanders, *Peoples Search: Discovering Unreached Peoples in Your Community and the North American Peoples Spectrum*, North American Mission Board, SBC (Alpharetta, GA: Church Planting Village, unpublished draft 2006, 2009), 4.

[2] David Garrison, *Church Planting Movements: How God Is Redeeming a Lost World* (Midlothian, VA: WIGTake Resources, 2004), 28.

[3] Ralph D. Winter, "The Concept of a Third Era in Missions," *Evangelical Missions Quarterly* (April 1981): 70–71.

Spiritually Informed People Understand Ethnic Diversity

God in his sovereignty determines where different ethnic groups (language groups) live every bit as much as God determines the recipe of culture and ethnicity recorded in the twenty-three chromosomes of our physical DNA (Acts 17:26–27). There are no accidents. God is responsible for bringing the nations close to his churches, even to your very neighborhood. This is the "nations" (*ta ethne*) of the Great Commission. With his infinitely large love for all people, God is constantly making the world a smaller place for his kingdom purposes—and he still expects us to go to the people. There is an overwhelming global need for those who have little or no access to the gospel (often referred to as Unreached People Groups/Unengaged People Groups) and yet there are also unreached and unengaged people groups close to us.

The most obvious example of ethnic-based outreach in the life of Christ is how he goes first to the Jews. (This statement does not diminish the truth that Jesus came as a Light to the Gentiles.) Matthew 10:6 records the twelve disciple's missionary assignment was initially for the "house of Israel." Jesus was specific here about not going to the Gentiles or the Samaritans (which he would do later). Jesus went first to the Jew, then the Gentile (Rom 1:16). Likewise, just like Jesus, Paul's pattern in Acts was to enter the synagogue first. Jesus's life and ministry along with stories of the book of Acts clearly demonstrates the gospel is for all peoples.

First Baptist Duluth, Georgia, experienced this firsthand. Pastor Mark Hearn remembers, "When we moved to Duluth six years ago, our neighbors were from India, Korea, Zimbabwe, and South Africa—a small snapshot of our surrounding community that opened my eyes to the need for our church to become more reflective of our community."[4] Pastor Mark began

---

[4] Mark Hearn, *How His Church Learned to Embrace Multicultural Ministry*, Baptist Press, accessed May 7, 2016, http://www.bpnews.net/49202/how-his-church-learned-to-embrace-multicultural-ministry; email and personal interviews with author, August 2011.

to lead the congregation to engage their very diverse community and now the church is becoming a beautiful mosaic of ethnicity reflecting their community's diversity. God brought spiritual understanding to the members of the church, and gave them the desire and tools to reach the nations in their own backyard.

For years sociologists have called North America a melting pot, but "mosaic" may be the best word to describe how people group themselves. Consider three language groupings that are likely in your community right now:

- Refugees fleeing other countries,
- Immigrant workers looking for a better life,
- International students attending college and graduate schools.

These ethnic groups are representative of unreached and unengaged populations across the world. International missions truly can begin without obtaining a visa or even boarding an airplane.

A church on mission will find ways to serve these peoples. Ask God to give you spiritual understanding and listen for his specific instructions for who and where. The following ideas are not novel but let them prime the pump for you: You can host international students in your home for a meal or invite them to participate in a holiday celebration. You can frequent a local ethnic restaurant or grocery store, making friends by learning their culture. You can volunteer at a local social service agency that works with refugees and immigrants. You can reach out to an ethnic family in your neighborhood or community and find areas of common interest. Make a friend first and at the right moment the conversation will turn toward the gospel. If we put ourselves in their shoes and sincerely offer our love, God's Spirit will work in their lives.

Spiritually Informed People Understand Location

In buying and selling real estate, it is about three things: location, location, and location. In Acts, it was about three things in regard to location—the cities, the cities, and the cities. They were a strategic priority in Acts because the reality is that most people lived in cities. The missionaries were led to urban locations with distinctive characteristics and personalities. John Stott, in his commentary on Acts writes, "It seems to have been Paul's deliberate policy to move purposefully from one strategic city-Centre to the next."[5] Just like in Acts, the church must move purposefully with the people. This does not imply that rural areas are insignificant in God's eyes. However, there is a strong flow of influence from cities to rural areas that cannot be ignored.

Though there were a few exceptions in the book of Acts, like the Ethiopian eunuch in the desert, the gospel most frequently went first to the population centers (the cities). In the Great Awakenings in America, it was places like New York and Chicago that became epicenters for a powerful move of God. With his home city of Chicago in mind, D. L. Moody said, "Cities are the centers of influence. Water runs downhill, and the highest hills in America are the great cities. If we can stir them we shall stir the whole country."[6]

A fresh movement is afoot as the North American Mission Board launched the Send North America national initiative in 2008. The aim was to penetrate the cities with the gospel through church planting. The idea was to have existing churches see the under-reached and under-served cities in need of the gospel in order that they would send church planters, teams, and volunteers to assist in planting multiplying churches. There has been and continues to be a tremendous response of planters and partnering churches working in these cities. New churches have been started and planting networks have been established in the thirty-two cities called Send

---

[5] John R. W. Stott, *The Message of Acts: The Spirit, the Church and the World* (Bible Speaks Today series) (Downers Grove, IL: Intervarsity Press, 1990), 293.

[6] Paul Dwight Moody and Arthur Percy Fitt, *The Shorter Life of D. L. Moody* (Chicago: Bible Institute Colportage Association, 1900), 79.

Cities. Check out the cities/focus areas and their planters along with how you and your church can be involved at www.namb.net/cities/.

The need for the church to move purposefully with the people is as important today as it was in Acts. A modern city in North America is made up of neighborhood clusters, urban core multifamily housing, suburbs with sprawling subdivisions, and outer rings of rural bedroom communities. Each location is a unique mission field and a place people call home. It is there that some folks most deeply identify and where you will be able to connect for the sake of the gospel through household networks of relationships. The location-based people groupings are persons who identify themselves predominantly by the place where they live: "I live at so and so" or "I'm from XYZ." These locations can include multifamily housing communities, such as apartments, mobile home parks, gated communities, and planned developments. They can be a city, town, or village. These locations can become some of the best places to reach the lost because people already cluster together in community—it's a natural place where the gospel can flow and make an impact. In rural villages and small towns, the people within the community are insiders to that location, and the person that learns how to "break into" that grouping can find a free channel for the gospel.

Are there practical things you and your church can do to engage people who predominately identify with their place? Yes, you can start by prayer driving or prayer walking a neighborhood or a city the Lord places on your heart. Schedule a visit with an apartment manager to ask how you can serve their residents and be ready to mobilize others to meet the needs. Record the points of interest within a village or small town and begin to visit the people (like the feed store, a restaurant, or the fire station). You might well discover where God is already at work.

Spiritually Informed People Understand Affinity Networks

People really enjoy their hobbies and interests. Sometimes, it becomes a major part of their identity or even their idol. Rather than fight this, an informed Christ follower will find a way to penetrate that affinity network for the sake of the gospel. It has been said, "We need all kinds of churches for all kinds of people." This is the beauty of the Body of Christ, so rich in diversity but one in heart and purpose. The amazing thing about affinity-based outreach is that you can spend time enjoying your own hobby or interest and it become ministry.

Jesus's most successful outreach was to an affinity group of tax collectors. The revenue collectors of Jesus's day were despised, which made them more open to geninue love and acceptance. Luke wrote, "All the tax collectors and sinners were approaching to listen to him. And the Pharisees and scribes were complaining, 'This man welcomes sinners and eats with them'" (Luke 15:1–2). This complaint prompted Jesus to tell three stories about the lost being found. God values lost people!

- Matthew the tax collector immediately walked away from his empty lifestyle to follow Jesus. He threw a party for Jesus and in turn extended an invite to all his network (Luke 5:29).
- Zacchaeus, another tax collector, climbed a tree to see Jesus. Jesus called him down, came to his house, and from that point everything began to radically change. Again, his network—those he cheated as well as fellow tax collectors—heard the gospel for the first time (Luke 19:1–10).

Jesus made friends with the tax collectors for the sake of the gospel (Luke 7:34). Have we ever been accused of being a friend of sinners and tax collectors? What affinity group might God be leading us to engage? Fair warning: it may cause some friction.

Affinity groupings cover a broad range of associations: any workplace, military personnel, bikers, cowboys, college students, classic car enthusiasts, quilting circles, scrapbookers, athletes, skateboarders, and outdoorsmen are only a few. Sometimes affinity-based outreaches eventually become new churches reaching a unique segment of the population because of their strong networks and common ground. The gospel can flow freely and find acceptance among these groups when placed in the right networks (recall David Garrision's definition of people groups).

There are some practical steps to reaching affinity-based people. First, identify what networks exist by surveying your friends from church about their hobbies, interests, and associations. Compile a list based on your findings and then find a way to become a missionary to the organization. Then participate in the affinities' special events and find creative ways to serve them. With any of these people groupings, missional effectiveness depends on authentic relationships based on love for God and other people. People can absolutely sense if you love them or not. Lastly, have a "whatever it takes" mindset to reach people. Think like the four men who tore through a rooftop to get a paralyzed man to Jesus (Mark 2:1–12). Like this man's friends, work hard to get people to Jesus and have faith in what he can do. If necessary, boldly take the roof off and be innovative in your methods of sharing the gospel.

Getting Started with Spiritual Understanding

With so many options of people groups to serve and preferences to remember, it can feel overwhelming to know where to start. But that is exactly the point of this chapter: the DNA principle of spiritual understanding—knowing who and where to go to—is received by divine revelation. We don't have to figure it out on our own or even make a best guess. God will guide us. Think of Philip and the Ethiopian in Acts 8, Peter and Cornelius in Acts 10, and Paul to the Macedonians in Acts 16. Each of these encounters occurred because God gave specific instructions to a believer.

Just as important, God expects that you and I and our churches will become students of our mission fields. It's a partnership. God guides our steps. Our responsibility is to learn our communities in such a way that we can share the gospel in a way others can hear it—with a sensitivity to their customs and heart languages. Our aim is to learn everything possible. The earliest followers observed the culture and used their real-time findings to more effectively share the gospel. In Acts 17, Paul already knew of their pantheon of gods. He already knew they had an altar "To an Unknown God" (v. 23). He intentionally studied the culture and then used his knowledge to teach the gospel.

For some of us, we need a reminder of how to hear God's direction. The great news is God made his sheep to hear his voice (John 10:27). We're created to hear him. What we have to do is slow down and listen expectantly for the heart of God. When we become still before the Lord, we can hear his whisper. Psalm 46:10 says: "Be still and know that I am the Lord." Slow down, friends. Busyness and distraction inhibit our ability to hear. Stop striving. The full verse is best translated as, "Stop your fighting, and know that I am God, exalted among the nations, exalted on the earth." Do you hear the whisper of God's heart for the *nations* and the *earth* there? The only One we need to please is Jesus, no one else. We please him when we focus on peoples and places in need of Christ. And remember, God is in control: nothing surprises him or sneaks up on him. We can trust Jesus in all things.

Conclusion

D. L. Moody, the great evangelist of his day, had an enormous heart for the lost. A man once asked Moody the secret of his success in leading people to Christ. Moody directed the man to his hotel window and asked, "What do you see?" The man looked down on the square and reported a view of crowded streets. Moody suggested he look again. This time the man mentioned seeing people: men, women, and children. Moody then directed him to look a third time. The man became frustrated that he was not seeing what Moody wanted him to. The great evangelist came to the window with watery eyes and said, "I see people going to hell without Jesus. Until you see people like that, you will not lead them to Christ."[7] People without Christ are dead men walking. Learn how to see with the compassionate eyes of Christ who saw the multitudes as sheep without a shepherd—helpless and harassed (Matt 9:36). Press in to God and ask who and where you are to serve and love them well.

---

[7] Raymond McHenry, *McHenry's Quips, Quotes and Other Notes* (Peabody, MA: Hendrickson, 1998), 85.

Acts Immersion

Acts Action Item

Follow God's lead to the people and places he wants you and your church to engage.

Culture Change: Complete DNA of a Church and Preaching

The expression of spiritual understanding leads to a holistic view of missions. The tendency for most churches and individual believers is to become myopic, only seeing your mission field as the people who are just like you. This is nothing more than incomplete DNA. Bob Roberts, pastor from Keller, Texas, writes:

> I don't think any church is a legitimate church if it's not engaged with the whole counsel of God, and the whole counsel of God is the whole world. When you say we're just here for our community, then basically you've said we're just a holy huddle. That's not a church. I don't think a church has the complete DNA of what God has for it if it's not engaged with the rest of the world.[8]

If pastors, leaders, and everyday Christ followers desire to see their church move to an Acts culture change, they must break out of the holy huddle and see the whole world as their mission field, starting at home and moving abroad. Our preaching must reflect God's heart for all peoples and call the world to Christ—the whole counsel of God. This will help create a church culture both locally and globally engaged in mission.

---

[8] Mark Galli, "Glocal Church Ministry: Bob Roberts Has an Idea That May Change American Congregations, If Not the World," *Christianity Today*, August 2, 2007, http://www.christianitytoday.com/ct/2007/july/30.42.html?type=next&number=21&id=46937&start=9.

Spiritual Understanding: Focus on Peoples and Places

Acts Character and Competence

Be...

- attentive—to hear the voice of God as he reveals our prejudices
- impartial—in sharing Jesus with all and starting churches for all peoples
- teachable—to discover all you can about a people group in order to overcome barriers and build bridges to the gospel

Know...

- that people group thinking can help us overcome barriers and personal prejudices to the gospel
- that Cornelius represented a spectrum of people group thinking—ethnicity, location, and affinity
- that people have a heart language to which the gospel can easily flow

Do...

- Prayerfully read the daily devotional "Acts Moment" and the Acts Bible readings below.
- Go to your rooftop (place of prayer) asking God to grant you spiritual understanding as it relates to unreached people groups.
- Ask God to fill you with his Holy Spirit afresh and anew to be his witness.
- Research a worldview regarding a people group (of your choosing) focused in your area (i.e. Google search).
- Commit to utilize the *ACTS Prayer Guide* at the weekly corporate prayer or your personal prayer time.

Acts Readings

Day 1: Acts 5:1–11
Day 2: Acts 5:12–16

Day 3: Acts 5:17–42
Day 4: Acts 6:1–7
Day 5: Acts 6:8–15

Acts Missionary Activity

Spiritual Understanding: People Group Discovery

This week, make plans to visit either an ethnic grocery store or an authentic ethnic restaurant. Kindly ask for permission to ask a few questions. Then ask these four questions of the people you encounter, and listen well:

1. What is your name?
2. What is your cultural background?
3. What is your religious background?
4. How many people of your ethnic group live in our city?

Thank them for taking the time to answer.

Reflection: What did you learn about the people groups in your city?

Spiritual Understanding in the Life of Christ

Jesus modeled spiritual understanding as he heightened the awareness that the gospel is for all peoples.

For Further Reading

- *Let the Nations Be Glad* by John Piper
- *Technicolor* by Mark Hearn
- *Communicating Christ Cross-Culturally* by David J. Hesselgrave

4

Spiritual Leadership: Identify and Nurture Missional Leaders
(Antioch)

*What you have heard from me in the presence of many witnesses,
commit to faithful men who will be able to teach others also.*
—2 Timothy 2:2

Spiritual leadership is moving people onto God's agenda.
—Henry Blackaby, *Spiritual Leadership*

> *Handwritten note: Leadership is not leading people to what I want, but what God wants*

What makes a leader: genetics or environment? Are leaders born or made? Is it nature or nurture? Before addressing this question, let's define a leader. In general, a leader is someone who has the capacity to influence their spheres and domains. A missional leader has the capacity to influence individual Christians and churches for the sake of God's mission. True Christlike leaders are practitioners and people of character who faithfully lead by example and integrity.

While there is certainly a genetic link to leadership, the truth is that leaders are both born *and* made—it's nature *and* nurture. What I find fascinating is that research suggests leadership is more environment than genetics. *Forbes* reported that "one study from *The Leadership Quarterly* on heritability (that is, the innate skills you bring to the table) and human development (what you learn along the way) estimated that leadership is 24 percent genetic and 76 percent learned."[1] The conclusion is you don't necessarily have to have the genetic material to be a leader. Leadership can be learned. This is good news for the church!

A church on mission knows that anything healthy will reproduce—that a church is measured by its sending capacity, not its seating capacity. Therefore, another strand of the spiritual DNA of a church is that *leaders intentionally identify and nurture new leaders*. It's not an afterthought; it's a prayerful, strategic part of the plan.

Consider Shubal Stearns. He was the pastor of Sandy Creek Baptist Church—a noteworthy, rural church in South Carolina established in 1755 on the heels of the First Great Awakening. The church had a passion for starting new churches and became a beachhead for a missional movement of church planting much like the church at Antioch. Robert Baker, a church historian, comments:

> The mother of all the Separate Baptists . . . which in 17 years, has spread branches as westward as the great river Mississippi; southward as far as Georgia; eastward to the sea and Chesapeake Bay; and northward to the waters of the Potomac; it in 17 years is become the mother, grandmother, great-grandmother to 42 churches, from which sprang 125 ministers.[2]

---

[1] Northwestern Mutual BRANDVOICE, "Are Leaders Born or Made?," *Forbes*, March 23, 2013, https://www.forbes.com/sites/northwesternmutual/2015/03/23/are-leaders-born-or-made/#6037dfc53e29.

[2] William Cathcart, *The Baptist Encyclopedia* (Philadelphia: Louis H. Everts, 1881), 917.

Sandy Creek intentionally identified and nurtured missional leaders from within their ranks and sent them out into the world. This is spiritual leadership.

Spiritual Leadership

What then is the crux of spiritual leadership? What are we nurturing toward? Much is written about leadership, but allow me to leave you with a few thoughts on spiritual leadership. If you add the descriptive word *spiritual* in front of *leadership*, the conversation changes dramatically. The old saying, "Everything rises and falls with leadership" is certainly true in the business world. However, in church life, this saying is woefully incomplete. Spiritual leadership is about *obedience to God*. Mark Clifton with the Send Network insightfully comments:

> I've heard this well intended remark over the years in relation to the health and growth of our churches. However, those of us with love of the fidelity of Scripture understand things do not rise and fall on our own leadership ability. Rather, they rise and fall on our obedience to Christ and the power of the Holy Spirit working in and through us. Everything rises and falls on our obedience.[3]

Think of Jesus in the Garden just before his crucifixion. His prayer was one of utter obedience: "Father, if you are willing, take this cup away from me—nevertheless, not my will, but yours, be done" (Luke 22:42). Jesus's will was completely surrendered to his Master's. The great need is for leaders who obey God at all cost and in all things personally and vocationally, including the commission to bring the gospel to all nations. The dire need is for "nevertheless" kind of leaders.

---

[3] Mark Clifton, in conversation with the author, August 2017. I am indebted to him for his insight into the liberating statement that everything does not rise and fall with leadership but with your obedience to God.

Spiritual leadership is also about *service*. In his book *Jesus on Leadership*, Gene Wilkes writes, "A servant leader serves the mission and leads by serving those on mission with him."[4] Jesus, with towel and basin in hand and a laser focus on his mission, is the ultimate model of servant leadership. Missional leadership is not a role but rather a goal of following Jesus's example. For Jesus, it meant service, suffering, and death. For us as servant leaders, it's an identification with Christ and our shared spiritual DNA in him. Missiologist John Mark Terry affirms, "The early church always looked back to Jesus as its model or example. Therefore, Jesus is not just the founder of missions; he is its prototype (Heb 12:1–2)."[5] Jesus gave us his pattern for missions in his life of service. Jesus said, "For even the Son of Man did not come to be served, but to serve, and to give his life as a ransom for many" (Mark 10:45). Follow the steps of the sovereign master of the universe who became a servant to all and obediently paid a king's ransom in order to make redemption possible for lost souls.

Finally, spiritual leadership is about *action*. Leaders pray and listen, but they don't stop there. They also act. Leaders at the church at Antioch were characterized by action. This was the kind of church with a hearty missionary culture that every church planter dreams of starting. They were wealthy with spiritual leaders like Barnabas, Saul, Agabus, Simeon, Lucius, Manaen, and a supporting cast of other unknown leaders. These folks had pressed in to the heart and mission of God and were actively engaged in the church and community. The end result was a church that grew both spiritually as well as numerically (Acts 11:21, 24). As you seek to identify potential leaders to nurture, look for the missional traits of obedience, service, and action.

---

[4] C. Gene Wilkes, *Jesus on Leadership: Discovering the Secrets of Servant Leadership from the Life of Christ* (Carol Stream, IL: Tyndale House, 1998), 18.

[5] John Mark Terry, Ebbie Smith, and Justin Anderson, *Missiology: An Introduction* (Nashville: B&H, 1998), 69.

Spiritual Leadership in Acts

Now that we've briefly discussed what spiritual leadership is, let's explore how the early church identified, nurtured, and sent out new leaders. Spiritual leadership in Acts can be evaluated by the four C's: calling, character, competency, and compatibility.[6]

Spiritually Nurtured People Lead Based on Calling

All that is known about the inception of the work at Antioch is that it began as a result of the persecution following Stephen's martyrdom (Acts 11:19–21). Some of the early followers went to Antioch to escape the persecution. As they did so, they naturally proclaimed the Lord Jesus to both the Jews and the Hellenists. God used these people to start the church at Antioch. They are nameless, known only to God, but they all chose to obey the call of God to follow Jesus and become fishers of men. Later, well-known leaders like Barnabas, Paul, and Agabus answered God's call and joined the work. Spiritual leadership begins with a personal call to follow God. It anchors us as spiritual leaders and provides us with the ability to endure all sorts of challenges along the way.

God also called and selected the Antioch missionary team. As the church worshipped together and fasted, "the Holy Spirit said, 'Set apart for me Barnabas and Saul for the work to which I have called them'" (Acts 13:2). God called specific people to do specific jobs in the early church and he does the same today. F. F. Bruce insightfully comments, "It is perhaps worth noticing that the two men who were to be released for what would nowadays be called missionary service overseas were the two

---

[6] Bill Hybels, *Courageous Leadership* (Grand Rapids: Zondervan, 2002), 177. The concept of the C's related to leaders have been espoused by numerous authors; one notable example is Bill Hybels's three C's: character, competence, and chemistry.

most eminent and gifted leaders in the church."[7] How willing are we to give away our best and brightest to missionary service? This is a mark of a healthy and secure church—not to mention an act of faith in God's ability to provide more leaders.

Spiritually Nurtured People Lead Based on Character

Spiritual leadership is also evaluated by a person's character. The church in Antioch set the standard for all future churches. Who labeled those first Christians in Antioch as "Christians" (Acts 11:26)? It was the watching lost culture. There were no job titles, business cards, or LinkedIn profiles to mark the disciples as Christ followers. Their defining trait was that their words and actions resembled Jesus Christ. They were the "real deal" before a lost world that desperately needed to hear and see God's love and holiness in action.

Barnabas, the Son of Encouragement, gives us an excellent picture of character. Scripture says he was:

- a good man, full of the Holy Spirit and faith;
- generous, selling personal property and giving the proceeds to the church;
- willing to believe and see God work in others (like Saul of Tarsus) when no one else would (Acts 9:26–31);
- a friend, mentor, and coach;
- a true servant, allowing Paul to assume the lead role on the missionary team (Acts 13:13, 46, 50);
- a courageous leader, risking his life on the missionary journeys (Acts 15:25–26);
- a man of humility, refusing to be worshiped as a god but faithfully pointing others to God;

---

[7] F. F. Bruce, *New International Commentary: Acts* (Grand Rapids: Eerdmans, 1998), 246.

- merciful toward the shortcomings of others, offering second chances (Acts 15:36–41); and
- a trustworthy man who, along with Paul, carried the offering back to Jerusalem (Acts 11:30).

Character matters with spiritual leadership. Samuel Brengle writes, "[Spiritual leadership] is not won by promotion but by many prayers and tears."[8] Christlike missionary character is often forged in the furnace of persecution, the trials of life, and on the battlefields of temptation. <u>God only gives out assignments when we have the character to match it.</u> Character really does matter in missions. John Shearer stated, "In every revival there is a re-emphasis of the Church's *missionary character.* Men return to Calvary, and the world is seen afresh through the eyes of Christ."[9] God is always at work shaping our missionary character to lead as Jesus led.

Spiritually Nurtured People Lead Based on Competency

Competency is also a component of spiritual leadership. Unlike calling and character—which a person either has or doesn't have—competency can be learned. Leaders are learners. The Holy Spirit empowers, equips, and teaches spiritual leaders to join in his mission according to his divine purposes. Each of the fivefold gifts in Ephesians was represented at the church in Antioch. After Barnabas arrived in Antioch originally, he soon "went to Tarsus to search for Saul, and when he found him he brought him to Antioch. For a whole year they met with the church and taught large numbers" (Acts 11:25–26). What was happening during that year with Barnabas and Saul? Barnabas was mentoring Saul and Saul was building his competency.

Moreover, it's worth noting how the gift of leadership is listed within the description of spiritual gifts in Romans: "If in exhorting, in exhortation;

---

[8] Samuel Logan Brengle, *The Soul-Winner's Secret* (London: Salvation Army, 1918), 22.

[9] John Shearer, *Old Time Revivals: How the Fire of God Spread in Days Now Past and Gone* (London: Pickering & Inglis, 1932).

giving, with generosity; leading, with diligence; showing mercy, with cheerfulness" (Rom 12:8). Leading takes diligence; it is hard work! Henry Blackaby describes leadership in terms of moving people onto God's agenda. Spiritual leadership is a gift that can be developed over time through diligence, learning how to influence people to follow God and his ways.

Spiritually Nurtured People Lead Based on Compatibility

Spiritual leadership is also evaluated by compatibility. Like those in Antioch, God expects his people to work together tirelessly in missional unity and alignment. Barnabas sought out Paul to help disciple the new believers in Antioch, encouraging his ministry to the Gentiles. Paul and Barnabas were linked together prior to Antioch, in Antioch, and soon they would be sent out on their first missionary journey together. They were great teammates.

Barnabas's and Paul's personalities, gifts, and talents were complementary in nature. Consider the differences: Barnabas was clearly connection oriented—he believed in Paul early on when the other disciples wouldn't. Paul was more driven by meeting objectives and removing any roadblocks to achieving them. They were both servant oriented but wired differently. Later, these differences led to a sharp disagreement over John Mark rejoining the team after he had deserted them on their first trip. Paul and Barnabas parted ways forming new teams: Paul with Silas and Barnabas with John Mark. Barnabas was the right person to develop John Mark; they were compatible. The beautiful end result was that John Mark became someone Paul depended on (2 Tim 4:11). Compatibility is critical in developing new leaders.

Spiritual Leadership Today

The Summit Church in Raleigh-Durham, North Carolina, is a classic twenty-first-century example of the DNA principle of spiritual leadership. Pastor J. D. Greear writes, "Sending is already in the DNA of any

Jesus-following church. *How* and where you are sent will be revealed by God's Spirit, but *that* you are sent has been declared once and for all in God's Word."[10] The Summit Church understands and practices this spiritual DNA principle. Pastor J. D. reminisces about a personal turning point, saying, "The church I pastor did not start out as a sending church. During my first years there, my focus was entirely on growing the church."[11] In his second year as pastor, when preaching through Acts, he concluded that the church would focus not on *gathering* but on *sending* to bless and reach the cities with the gospel.

Today, Summit is sending missionaries around the world and across North America. Pastor J. D. now describes the church as a leadership pipeline, one that challenges people to be leaders and then equips them to answer God's call to service. They continue to send out their people as leaders utterly secure in the Lord's provision to bring new leaders to their church. It becomes multiplication in motion when the Holy Spirit does the sending.

A Word of Caution

Before moving on, there is one last "C" word pertaining to spiritual leadership to avoid—*cloning*. Dolly the sheep made news in 1997 as the first mammal to be cloned.[12] Spiritual leaders are not meant to be carbon copies of one another. We're not all supposed to wear the same clothes or pump our hands vigorously when we preach or do evangelistic outreaches with the same flavor. God is utterly intentional about how we're wired and what we've experienced and learned in life. There's a reason for that: we're all

---

[10] J. D. Greear, *Gaining by Losing: Why the Future Belongs to Churches That Send* (Grand Rapids: Zondervan, 2015), 51.

[11] Greear, 41.

[12] BBC, "1997: Dolly the Sheep is Cloned," On This Day, accessed June 19, 2014, http://news.bbc.co.uk/onthisday/hi/dates/stories/february/22/newsid_4245000/4245877.stm.

called to unique places. Don't make the mistake of developing new leaders to look just like you or operate just like you.

Perhaps even more importantly, you and I are not to clone anyone else in our behavior either. We church leaders often struggle with insecurity. We want to be employed! We may find our identity in a title or in achieving certain attendance numbers. It can be all too easy for us to try to be like a more "successful" pastor or leader.

David, the shepherd boy who became king, is a great example of the four C's of spiritual leadership and one who also avoided cloning anyone else. Observe the calling, character, and competency when he said, "He *chose* David his servant and took him from the sheep pens; he brought him from tending ewes to be shepherd over his people Jacob—over Israel, his inheritance. He shepherded them with a *pure heart* and guided them with his *skillful hands*" (Ps 78:70–72, emphasis added). For compatibility, David had Jonathan and all his mighty men (1 Sam 20:1–42; 2 Sam 23:8–39). Remember what's true. God created you uniquely for such a time as this. God no sooner made a random, thoughtless match between you and your church context than God does for a parent and a child. Be who God created you to be and stay the course to a growing walk with Jesus.

Conclusion

Spiritual leaders are people of obedience, service, and action. Michael Slaughter, in his book *Church Unique*, writes:

> Spiritual leaders are the carriers of God's DNA in the church, the shapers of a church's vision and core values. They are influencers of what the church embodies. . . . The key to radical discipleship is the development of trainer coaches that carry the DNA to the edges of the movement.[13]

---

[13] Michael Slaughter, *Unlearning Church* (Nashville: Abingdon, 2008), 79.

It is imperative that you, as pastor or church leader, practice what you preach about spiritual leadership and intentionally nurture new leaders. Spiritual leadership is the missional tipping point for an everyday Christ follower, for a Christian family, and for a local church to obey God and move onto his agenda. This kind of leadership is the key to the success of a church in his eyes. If your church is not experiencing an increase in new disciples, new leaders, and new church plants, ask God to grow you in this area. God can use you to lead the way in creating a sending culture in your church and beyond.

Acts Immersion

Acts Action Item

Invest in identifying and nurturing missional leaders in your life and the life of your church.

Culture Change: Leadership and Serving Others

Even the business world gets it. Peter Drucker, known as the father of modern management, wrote, "Leaders are those who have followers."[14] Jim Collins, author of *Good to Great*, speaks of "Level 5 leaders," who are "a study in duality: modest and willful, humble and fearless."[15] But perhaps no one in the business world said it better than Robert Greenleaf who wrote:

> The Servant-Leader is servant first. It begins with the natural feeling that one wants to serve. Then conscious choice brings one to aspire to lead. The difference manifests itself in the care taken by the servant—first to make sure that the other people's highest priority needs are being served.[16]

This sounds like Jesus. In fact, he said the one who leads must be willing to serve (Matt 20:25–28). The Antioch church exemplified a healthy culture of spiritual leadership through serving. Truett Cathy of Chick-fil-A built a flourishing business by creating a culture of second-mile customer service. Let everything you do in your church be characterized by going the extra

---

[14] Peter Drucker, "Managing Oneself," *Harvard Business Review* 77, no. 2 (1999): 65–74.

[15] Jim Collins, *Good to Great: Why Some Companies Make the Leap and Others Don't* (New York: HarperBusiness, 2001), 22.

[16] Robert K. Greenleaf, *Servant Leadership* (Mahwah, NJ: Paulist Press, 1997), 7.

mile and serving others. If you do that, the culture of your church *will* change—and that is spiritual leadership.

Note: The spiritual DNA principles are mirrored in the business world (See appendix 9)

Acts Character and Competence

Be . . .

- healthy—consistently examine yourselves for leadership deficiencies
- sent—to share Jesus and start churches for all peoples and places
- encouraged—by discovering a leader who you can multiply yourself through
- teachable—take the posture of a humble learner

Know . . .

- that spiritual leaders move people onto God's agenda
- that Antioch sent out their best and brightest on mission
- that a healthy church is measured by its sending capacity
- that Jesus modeled spiritual leadership as he led his followers, and so did the church at Antioch

Do . . .

- Commit to and complete the Acts daily reading plan.
- Prayerfully read the daily devotional *"Acts Moment."**
- Seek out potential leaders considering calling, character, competency, and compatibility.
- Ask God to fill you with his Holy Spirit afresh and anew to be a spiritual leader.
- Take time to evaluate your spiritual leadership in light of the leaders of Antioch.
- Commit to utilize the *ACTS Prayer Guide* at the weekly corporate prayer or your personal prayer time.

Acts Readings

Day 1: Acts 7:1–53
Day 2: Acts 7:54–8:3
Day 3: Acts 8:4–8:8
Day 4: Acts 8:9–25
Day 5: Acts 8:26–40

Acts Missionary Activity

Spiritual Leadership: Identify Potential Leaders

This week, ask God to lead you to affirm a person for their leadership efforts in serving. Look for the unlikely leader, perhaps someone who serves in a behind-the-scenes capacity. Write down two or three things that you observe in this person that demonstrates their current or potential leadership. Call them or send a note encouraging them. In your prayer time, ask God to reveal his will to that person in developing them into an even greater, effective spiritual leader.

Reflection: What was it about the person that made you see them as a potential leader?

Spiritual Leadership in the Life of Christ

Jesus modeled spiritual leadership as he led his followers to be kingdom influencers in obedience, service, and action.

For Further Reading

- *Spiritual Leadership* by Oswald Sanders
- *Servant Leadership* by Gene Wilkes
- *The Case for Antioch* by Jeff Iorg

Spiritual Synergy: Work Together for Greater Impact
(Philippi)

I planted, Apollos watered, but God gave the growth.
—1 Corinthians 3:6

In God's economy, the team was and is vital to the propagation of the gospel and the multiplication of disciples, leaders and churches.
—J. D. Payne, *Apostolic Church Planting*

We see the undeniable power of synergy throughout nature. During migration, a flock of geese fly in V-formation and rotate leadership at its point. In so doing, they create upward air currents for one another and synergistically increase capacity in the flock's flying range that would be impossible if each goose flew alone. The act of synergy causes exponentially more resources to be available and far greater goals to be achievable. Their V-formation also allows them to have a good line of sight for effective communication and coordination with one another.

Scientists have no real explanation for why geese act synergistically, rotating out of the lead, because it really does seem counter to the "selfish gene" of DNA—survival of the fittest. Yet, these geese seem to be doing it for the mutual benefit of the flock. Some researchers ascribe the behavior to a genetic predisposition through a social dilemma. A study of the Royal Veterinary College concluded, "This study is a beautiful demonstration of how genomes and behavioral traits often need to be understood outside the context of an animal's immediate phenotype. When it comes to evolution, it's clear that individuals can benefit without being 'selfish.'"[1] There is no doubt God innately created geese with the ability to help one another, not an evolutionary process. Geese choose to cooperate for the good of the whole and their example gives us a vivid picture of synergistic teamwork in the natural realm and in the kingdom of God.

We see synergy in its purest form in the Triune God. This is the apex of spiritual synergy—the Father, the Son, and the Holy Spirit all working together to seek and save the lost. We see it too in Jesus's life as he prayerfully selects and travels with the twelve (Mark 3:13–18). Jesus taught synergy, or the power of teamwork, everywhere he went, including sending the disciples out two by two with the seventy and the twelve (Luke 10:1 and Mark 6:7).

Spiritual synergy comes from the understanding of co-laboring with God and with one another. Paul said, "I planted, Apollos watered, but God gave the growth. . . . We are God's coworkers" (1 Cor 3:6–9). The word rendered *coworker* is where the English word *synergy* is derived—a combination of work and energy. In other words, we can understand synergy as the whole that is greater than the sum of its parts.[2] We accomplish far more working together than we do on our own. The spiritual synergy of team was and still is God's special ingredient to an effective church.

---

[1] George Dvorsky, "Why Birds Take Turns at the Front When Flying in V-Formation," i09, February 3, 2015, https://io9.gizmodo.com/why-birds-take-turns-at-the-front-when-flying-in-v-form-1683465294.

[2] *Merriam-Webster Online Dictionary*, s.v. "synergy," accessed August 15, 2014, https://www.merriam-webster.com/dictionary/synergy.

Dysfunctional Synergy: Together Everyone Accomplishes Less

In many churches today we experience the exact opposite of synergy. In fact, it's possible your experience is more like what Ryan Hartwig and Warren Bird describe in their book *Teams That Thrive*. Writing about their insightful book, Bird had this to say:

> If it's true that teamwork makes the dream work, why do groups that come together in our churches to accomplish Kingdom tasks too often experience dismal results? Too much of the "teamwork" we experience in church (and elsewhere) conjures up images of wandering discussions, unresolved friction, wasted time, pooled ignorance, ineffective decision-making and frustrated group members—all in spite of good intentions regarding the potential of working together.[3]

The genetic mutation of synergy is akin to entropy. It's an ever-decreasing effectiveness or trend to death and disorder where the whole is actually smaller than the sum of its parts. Low performance teams actually increase in weakness.

Entropy is one of the main reasons the work suffers in so many churches. It is often caused by people who choose to fly solo in missions. This spiritual insularity develops because of an unhealthy focus on individualism and independence rather than a dependence on God and an interdependence on one another. At its core, entropy is a form of selfishness and pride.

This does not have to be your experience. If the idea of entropy sounds eerily familiar, prayerfully examine your teams. Pat MacMillan defines *team* as "a group of people committed to a common purpose who choose to cooperate in order to achieve exceptional results."[4] The common purpose is advancing God's kingdom. If a team in your church is divided or

---

[3] Warren Bird, "Solving the Reasons Church Teams Too Often Fail," Leadership Network, March 16, 2015, http://leadnet.org/solving-the-reasons-church-teams-too-often-fail/.

[4] Pat MacMillan, *The Performance Factor: Unlocking the Secrets of Teamwork* (Nashville: B&H, 2001), 29.

under-functioning, consider ways to form new compatible teams wholly dependent on the Holy Spirit and interdependent on one another. There is great joy to be had when we operate synergistically, accomplishing more together than we could on our own . . . even the impossible with God.

Teams on Mission Together in Philippi

The Philippian church birth story illustrates some of the best practices of biblical teamwork and synergy, and, ultimately, gospel advance (Acts 16:6–34). Acts 16 marks the beginning of the "we" sections of Acts (Acts 16:10; 20:5–21:17 and 27:1–28:16).[5] Before this chapter, Luke communicated primarily as a historian, but now he shifts to write from the perspective of an eyewitness observer and team member. The very word *we* is a clear "togetherness indicator" of team. They did life together. This "we" included Luke, Silas, and, more than likely, Timothy. Although Paul and Silas were imprisoned, one can speculate Luke and Timothy were not too far away (Acts 16:1–10). This was a tight group of believers. They traveled, ate, laughed, played, and worked together as a cohesive unit—always focused intently on their mission with God. This "one another" team culture of the early church was characterized by shared community, healthy collaboration, and consistent missional alignment.[6] This same tight-knit culture applies to us today. Although not an exhaustive list, consider the following traits of these synergistic teams in Philippi and what they mean for our teams today.

Spiritually Synergistic People Discern God's Will Together

Notice that the team did not automatically go to Philippi. The Holy Spirit desires to direct his missionaries to the next destination. In order for this to happen, we have to be in tune with his leadings. The team could have gone to

---

[5] Bruce, *New International Commentary: Acts*, 7 (see chap 4., n. 7).
[6] Bob Burton, *Spiritual DNA Workbook: Church Genome Project* (Nashville: B&H Academic, 2019), 123–24.

Asia or Bithynia, but God stopped them from doing so. Instead, God led them by an undeniable vision to Macedonia. There are good indications the gospel did eventually go to Bithynia as Peter mentions the believers there (1 Pet 1:1–2), but it wasn't in this moment. God's timing truly does make all the difference.

Look also at verse 10: "After he had seen the vision, we immediately made efforts to set out for Macedonia, *concluding* that God had called us to preach the gospel to them" (Acts 16:10, emphasis added). The word "concluding" speaks of the need to work through decisions together as a team (Acts 16:10). Ken Blanchard writes, "None of us is as smart as all of us."[7] That is the beauty of collective wisdom. When it comes to spiritual discernment a synergistic team listens to God and discovers his will together. The first step Paul took before going to Philippi was to share with the team the vision of the Macedonian Call. Then they concluded *together* that God was directing them there (Acts 16:10). God will direct our teams to the next missional step if we seek him together.

Spiritually Synergistic People Evangelize the Lost Together

Evangelism and discipleship best happen together through a team because of increased accountability, mutual encouragement, and shared responsibilities. Paul and Silas made their way to the place of prayer together and discovered Lydia, a seller of purple cloth. Soon after, the Lord opened her heart to the gospel and she received the gift of salvation. Luke recorded that her whole household came to faith. But God was not finished in Philippi after their first encounter. God brought deliverance to a fortune-teller servant girl, in bondage not only to an earthly master but also to the devil. This brought about an uproar in the city, and Paul and Silas were immediately thrown into jail. God provided the next evangelistic opportunity after God released them through an earthquake. The Philippian jailer was ready to end

---

[7] Ken Blanchard, *The Heart of a Leader: Insights on the Art of Influence* (Colorado Springs: David C. Cook, 1999), 21.

his life. However, Paul intervened by sharing the hope of the gospel, and the jailer believed in the Lord along with his whole household (Acts 16:16–34).

Imagine for a moment if you were the one in Philippi, but were all alone. Imagine if you were perhaps trained, experienced, and gifted in evangelism but not in dealing with the demonic. Perhaps you were able to encourage others but, left on your own, your spirits dwindled in prison. Or perhaps doubt would have created a fog in your perception without a brother to remind you of God's truth. How effective would you be? Our evangelism is far more effective in the long term with a team than on our own. God has DNA hard-wired us for team.

Spiritually Synergistic People Endure Hardship Together

Synergy does not always make everything easy, but it does make adversities bearable, even exciting. Paul and Silas faced opposition in Philippi. While in chains, they prayed and sang to the Lord in that dark place. They turned an unjust, impossible circumstance into worship! Paul had companions who stayed with him through thick and thin. Read the last chapter of Romans—a long band of friends and co-laborers in Christ (Rom 16:1–27). In fact, Paul would close almost all his other epistles by naming friends and co-laborers in the gospel. The biblical commentator A. T. Robertson lists thirty-one of Paul's fellow laborers who served together with him in the missionary endeavors.[8] We've all experienced the life-giving impact of sharing dark times with brothers and sisters. Friendship is beautiful, but friendship forged through kingdom partnership is unsurpassed.

Spiritually Synergistic People Experience God's Miraculous Work Together

In their journey to and at Philippi, Paul and Silas experienced the miraculous together. They experienced divine direction through the Macedonian

---

[8] A. T. Robertson, *Studies in the New Testament* (Nashville: Sunday School Board SBC, 1915), 183.

vision. Paul and Silas literally saw people transformed by the gospel before their eyes. They saw demons cast out and people come to faith, as well as experienced a miraculous jailbreak before even more people came to faith. There is *nothing* ordinary about working together on God's agenda. Working together in partnership with God is the greatest adventure we can ever have. What our world needs is more people setting aside the American dream and all its trappings in order to live a God-sized adventure on mission with Christ.

A Twenty-First-Century Example of Spiritual Synergy

New Hope Christian Fellowship in Honolulu, Hawaii, is a church that emphasizes spiritual synergy. Founding Pastor Wayne Cordeiro has led the charge to unite as teams for greater mission impact. He writes in *Doing Church as a Team*, "Church numbers are insignificant when every individual is not involved. However, if the team members work together as one toward a single, clearly defined goal, anything is possible, and everyone shares in the joys and rewards of success!"[9] The crucial art of reproducing discipleship teams is the heart and soul of their strategy because they practice shared leadership. There are three words that describe their approach to doing church through relationship building, servant leadership, and discipleship teams that rapidly reproduce: welcome, equip, and send.

New Hope learned how to operate synergistically from the moment the church launched in a public school in 1983. They intentionally started with seven teams based on ministry function. They strategically partnered with their local high school, serving them together to upgrade the building and sound system as well as making other improvements. What distinguishes New Hope is their methodology for reproducing discipleship teams. "The number 10 is the regulatory and optimal number for groups. They use a formula $1 + 4 \times 2 = 10$ to identify one facilitator (team leader),

---

[9] Wayne Cordeiro, *Doing Church as a Team: The Miracle of Teamwork and How It Transforms Churches* (Ventura, CA: Regal Books, 2004), 7, 91.

four persons who bring complementary gifts, and any available spouses to form discipleship teams with a maximum of ten persons."[10] Pastor Wayne continues, "One of the most critical keys to doing church as a team is to build an ever-increasing core of servant-leaders. No pastor was designed to do church alone. . . . When people in the church make decisions consistent with the core values, you achieve a wonderful synergy and a culture of balance and truth."[11] This is spiritual synergy. God has raised this church to be a great mission force for reaching people with the gospel and planting new churches throughout the Pacific Rim.

Conclusion

Naval jets take off and land from aircraft carriers with amazing precision. On the flight deck you can see various crews and an air traffic control tower ensuring things run smoothly, with every necessary skill set present to keep the carrier in battle-ready posture. Underneath the short airstrip is a multistory synergistic team of support. While the jets taking off are super impressive, the landings are even more so. They come in at a high rate of speed; land on a moving target; and come to a sudden stop, caught by what is called an arresting wire—an incredibly strong steel cable made up of smaller strands of steel wire twisted around a core.

Everyone knows that the strength of a rope or cable is the intertwined nature of many smaller cords. This is what synergistic teams achieve: an uncanny strength to do far more together than what any one individual can. Solomon's words hold true that "a cord of three strands is not quickly broken" (Eccl 4:9–12). A church on mission builds synergistic teams to achieve incredible kingdom results.

---

[10] Rocky Mountain Ministry Network of the Assemblies of God, "Paul's Missionary Band Serves as an Excellent Metaphor for 21st Century Ministry" (pdf), accessed December 27, 2018, https://www.rmdc.org/wp-content/uploads/2018/09/Church-Planting-Pauls-Missionary-band-serves-as-an-excellent-metaphor-for-21st-century-ministry.pdf.

[11] Cordeiro, *Doing Church as A Team*, 177.

Acts Immersion

Acts Action Item

Choose to work together as a synergistic team in your life and the life of your church.

Culture Change: Team Synergy and Missional Small Groups

Disciples do life together and they do missions together. It is the shared mission that makes a difference in barriers to fellowship because the mission of the gospel is greater than personal preferences and sacred cows of ministry. Love for God and love for one another is the standard. Todd Engstrom writes:

> For us, a missional community is not just a [B]ible study, it's not just a fellowship group, it's not just a social action club, it's not just a support group, and it's certainly not just a weekly meeting.
>
> Healthy missional communities include all of those things over time, but it's a family of missionaries learning to follow Jesus in every area of their lives.[12]

A church culture goes adrift when there is no sense of accountability to the mission and a biblical Christian lifestyle. A life of faith is about living like a team of missionaries. Change the accountability level and change the missional culture of the church.

---

[12] Todd Engstrom, "What Is a Missional Community?—More than a Bible Study," *Todd Engstrom* blog, March 25, 2013, http://toddengstrom.com/2013/03/25/what-is-a-missional-community-more-than-a-bible-study/.

Acts Character and Competence

Be . . .

- people and task oriented—as a companion and coworker in ministry, relationships are everything to getting the task completed
- aligned—know your assignment on the team and work together
- flexible—to serve on a team you will need to give in and adjust as the Lord leads the team
- engaged—help the team make better decisions, hearing God's voice

Know . . .

- that spiritual synergy empowers the team to exponentially accomplish more through God's power
- that Paul and his companions formed an interdependent team to share Christ and start churches
- that in church planting and missions, team is the most effective way to work
- that Jesus modeled spiritual synergy by choosing his team (disciples), sending them out two by two, and by His relationship with the Father and the Holy Spirit

Do . . .

- Commit to and complete the Acts daily reading plan.
- Prayerfully read the daily devotional "*Acts Moment.*"*
- Form a team to begin praying about how to be involved in God's mission.
- Evaluate each team that you are a part of in church; how do they function according to the biblical standards of *team*?
- Ask God to fill you with his Holy Spirit afresh and anew to be a part of a missional team.
- Commit to utilize the *ACTS Prayer Guide* at the weekly corporate prayer or your personal prayer time.

Acts Readings

Day 1: Acts 9:1–19
Day 2: Acts 9:20–31
Day 3: Acts 9:32–43
Day 4: Acts 10:1–8
Day 5: Acts 10:9–23

Acts Missionary Activity

Spiritual Synergy: Power of Team Formation

This week, enlist two other people from your church to form a team to do a service project (for example: work for a food pantry, a homeless shelter, or for neighbors in need). As a team, ask God to direct you to the project. Once you have determined place and project, make assignments based on giftedness. Allow all the team to share their ideas and input. Head out the door and go get the job accomplished for God's glory.

Reflection: What did you learn about team formation and spiritual synergy?

Spiritual Synergy in the Life of Christ

Jesus modeled spiritual synergy by choosing his team (disciples), sending them out two by two, and by His relationship with the Father and the Holy Spirit.

For Further Reading

- *Doing Church as a Team* by Wayne Cordeiro
- *High Performance Teams* by Pat MacMillan
- *Leading the Team-Based Church* by George Cladis

6

Spiritual Receptivity: Discover Persons of Peace
(Philippi)

Whatever house you enter, first say, "Peace to this household." If a person of peace is there, your peace will rest on him; but if not, it will return to you.
—Luke 10:5–6

I call them "first domino" people, who start a chain reaction for the Kingdom. When they become Christian, others within their "Oikos" (relational network) do so as well, often almost immediately.
—Neil Cole, *Organic Church*

Do you believe everyone has a genetic capacity to believe in God? In his book *The God Gene*, Dean H. Hamer presents his thesis for the existence of a genetic propensity toward belief in God, or at least a spiritual belief. It is akin to a biological mechanism. He calls it, "A genetic predisposition for spiritual belief that is expressed in response to, and shaped by, personal experience and the cultural environment."[1] It's fascinating genetic theory to be sure, but whether or not we agree with it, finding persons of peace or "first dominos" is a kingdom key for the multiplication of disciples and new churches. Spiritual receptivity, or the discovery of persons of peace, is the next strand of DNA.

Persons of peace are those God has prepared ahead of time to hear the gospel or who express an openness to the gospel. This often means that persons of peace welcome believers. They will more than likely have an influential network of relationships. Persons of peace are welcoming to you and I and serve as a gospel witness. These people can become a missional entry point into a family, neighborhood, or community. They may want to assist believers in some way like making connections or they may want to spend time with believers. The DNA principle of *spiritual receptivity* is a commitment to discover and engage strategic persons of peace for the sake of the gospel. According to the Scriptures, it is entirely possible to discover individuals as well as whole networks of people whom the Holy Spirit has already been working on. Think of Cornelius and the Ethiopian eunuch that we've already discussed. Their hearts were opened and turned to God *before* they heard the good news of Jesus.

Reaching out first to persons of peace is a powerful strategy for sowing the gospel. Throughout Acts persons of peace were found in a receptive cultural environment—most often homes, synagogues, or the marketplace. These points of interest were consistently points of entry into new communities for Paul and his companions to reach those God had already been preparing to receive the gospel. It was his usual custom and missional strategy to go to the synagogue first in search of receptive peoples (Acts 17:2).

During the First Great Awakening, God used John Wesley through his so called "new methods" which were really the old methods of spiritual receptivity. The gospel went by horseback with circuit rider preachers looking for persons of peace. These gospel riders helped facilitate the founding

---

[1] Dean H. Hamer, *The God Gene: How Faith Is Hardwired into Our Genes* (New York: Random House, 2004), 8.

of many churches. Historians S. T. Kimbrough and Kenneth G. C. Newport write about Wesley's practice of this spiritual DNA:

> Some homesteaders invited him to a meal and overnight lodging. While visiting the dwelling, he spoke with each person about matters of soul and led the family in worship. If the householder agreed, the preacher added the cabin to his circuit as a "preaching station." Before the preacher's next visit, the householder invited neighbors to attend the upcoming service. Soon the circuit rider organized class meetings, led by capable lay people.[2]

God prepared select homesteaders to be persons of peace before the circuit riders ever arrived. Then God used these open hearts to impact their household and existing networks of relationships.

The Purpose of Spiritual Receptivity

Spiritual receptivity is one of the ways God maximizes our efforts. God first redirected Paul's team away from Asia and Bithynia, sending them instead to some very specific persons of peace in Philippi. No doubt surprising to them were the first people they discovered: religious women of commerce gathered by the river to worship at the place of prayer. The team of missionaries went to the place designated for worship because there was not a synagogue in the Roman colony of Philippi. Again, Paul's custom was to go to the synagogue first and he almost always found receptive people there. But in Philippi, God led the team to this riverbank of receptivity—his way of getting them before the right people. Much like how Facebook has capitalized on the six degrees of separation in our modern world, seeking out persons of peace led to a domino effect for spreading the gospel. So how exactly does God use spiritual receptivity to maximize our efforts? There are four ways.

---

[2] S. T. Kimbrough and Kenneth G. C. Newport, *The Manuscript Journal of Rev. Charles Wesley, M.A.* (Sherbourne, UK: Kingswood Books, 2007), 2:13.

Spiritual Receptivity Maximizes Present Realities

The reality is not everyone will receive us or the gospel. Jesus even instructed the disciples to shake the dust off their feet as a symbolic act against a community when its people were unreceptive (Matt 10:14; Mark 6:11; Luke 9:5; 10:11). In fact, they did this very thing in Antioch of Pisidia (Acts 13:51). God can maximize our efforts by sending us to fertile soil, not hardened or desert soil. This does not preclude the fact that he uses his people in the hard and desert soils. Missional engagement is the only way to find the open and prepared peoples.

The beginning of the church in Philippi is a stunning example of all ten strands of the spiritual DNA of a church on mission (see appendix 6). In fact, Acts 16 was believed to be an early manual on how to establish a new church.[3] It contains Paul's and his team's pattern and approach to church planting:

1. Enter the community—interact to measure receptivity (vv. 6–13)
2. Evangelize the lost—share the gospel with those who will listen (vv. 14–31)
3. Equip the new believers—make disciples, baptize, and teach (vv. 32–34)
4. Encourage the believers—secure leadership (vv. 35–40, implied by the use of the word *they*. A case can be made for Luke and possibly Timothy staying behind. Luke reverted back to the third person, and this possible action aligns with the previous pattern of appointing elders in every city—Acts 14:23)[4]
5. Exit the community—travel to the next place and repeat (v. 40)

The team also wrote to the churches and periodically returned to them in person to strengthen and encourage the believers (Acts 14:21–22). Paul's

---

[3] E. Elbert Smith, *Church Planting by the Book* (Fort Washington, PA: CLC Publications, 2015), 9–14.

[4] Bruce, *New International Commentary: Acts*, 38–39 (see chap 4, n. 7).

team gives us a beautiful example to seek out receptive audiences. Kingdom maximizers understand this and leverage the simplicity of God's ways that lead to greater gospel influence and church expansion.

Before continuing any further, let's briefly look at how to identify persons of peace. What do these people look like? In his book *Organic Church*, Neil Cole succinctly describes them:

1. Persons of peace are people of receptivity. They are open to the gospel message of the person and peace of Christ.
2. They are people with relational connections. They know a lot of people and are an important part of the community, for better or worse.
3. They are people of reputation (either good or bad). They possess a reputation whether it is good or bad.[5]

Lydia, the jailer, and possibly even the slave girl from Acts 16 fit this matrix. Other notable examples from Acts are the Ethiopian eunuch, Cornelius, Aquila, Priscilla, Crispus, and Justus. These persons of peace are a sample of the good soil Jesus spoke about in his parable. Some lost people are more open to the Holy Spirit's work in their life than others. Our task is to seek them out and be sensitive to God's activity in their lives.

Spiritual Receptivity Maximizes Relational Networks

Relational networks are difference makers. The missionary team found a riverside prayer meeting a receptive place. This led to meeting Lydia—the first person of peace in Philippi. Luke recorded how the Lord graciously opened her heart to receive and believe the gospel. Right then, as new believers in Christ, she and her household (part of her relational network) were all baptized in that same river (Acts 16:14–15). Lydia was also a well-connected business woman and seller of purple clothing from Thyatira. The

---

[5] Cole, *Organic Church*, 181–84.

sharing of the gospel and discipleship occurred through her existing spheres of influence. She warmly welcomed the missionary team and others into her home—and it's likely she hosted the gatherings for the Philippian church. Also, the mention of her roots in Thyatira may even indicate that Lydia played a part in the future establishment of this church through her business contacts (Acts 16:14; Rev 2:18).

It was common in Acts for people to come to Christ in groups, often described as *oikos* or "household"—a primary example of a relational network. Missiologist Thom Wolf writes,

> An oikos is a social system composed of those related to each other through common ties and tasks. The New Testament oikos included members of the nuclear family, but extended to dependents, slaves and employees. Oikos members often lived together, but always sensed a close association with each other. And note this carefully, the oikos constituted the basic social unit by which the early church grew, spreading the Good News of Jesus Christ, the risen Lord.[6]

In Philippi, the word *oikos* was used about both Lydia and the jailer, and their whole households readily came to faith in Christ (Acts 16:15, 31).

Notice two important lessons to engaging persons of peace through the missionary team's encounter with Lydia.

1. Start with prayer. Ask God where to go and then expect to find the people of peace. This is about faith in God and believing he is already at work in the fields. (John 5:19–20; Acts 16:9)
2. Notice the team's posture. The way to find a person of peace is to slow down. Take the time to get to know this person. Be willing to accept their invitations. Go to their homes. Go to their restaurants. Paul was willing to interact with people anywhere the Spirit led

---

[6] Thomas A. Wolf, "Oikos Evangelism: The Biblical Pattern," Apostolic Information Service, February 8, 2008, https://www.apostolic.edu/oikos-evangelism-the-biblical-pattern/.

him. Watch to insure you and your church aren't ignoring your neighbors.

By beginning with prayer and living with an open posture, God will lead you to the people of peace in your community.

The best story in Scripture of a person of peace (in my opinion) is Jesus's encounter with a woman at Jacob's well in Samaria (John 4). Her relational network is the entire village of Sychar! What did Jesus do? He slowed down and intentionally interacted with this woman. In so doing, Jesus was a target for criticism. She was a woman with a bad reputation from a despised people group. But he shared with her the life-changing gospel and she was immediately changed. Instead of going to the well to draw water, she put down her pot and took the living water to her village. God changed her agenda to his missonal agenda. Her relational network came to believe that Jesus was the Messiah because of her witness.

Spiritual Receptivity Maximizes the Liberated Life

God is still at work today setting people free from bondage, abuse, and addictions. When someone is transformed by God and delivered, the effect on that person—and the ripple effect on their community—is nothing short of miraculous. We often overlook the slave girl in Acts 16, a parallel picture of human trafficking in the first century. God used Paul to command the evil spirit to depart from her. She was freed from the demonic and nothing more is known of her in Scripture.

In the life of Christ, there is a similar story about a demoniac from the regions of the Gerasenes and with him we know the rest of the story. He was known only as the man of the tombs. Before he met Christ, peace would have been the very last word used to describe him as he was possessed by a legion of violent demons. Jesus engaged him, confronted the evil within him, and cast the demons into a herd of swine. The herd immediately ran off the edge of a cliff and drowned in the sea. The people of the community were filled with great fear: not only was their source of income (the pigs) dead, but the former demoniac was now at peace—sitting, clothed, and in his right mind (Mark 5:1–20). As mind boggling as it may seem, many people are more comfortable with the status quo than the liberating work of God in a person's life. Even believers can be more concerned about the next barbeque than seeking or saving the lost.

The man of the tombs became a person of peace. Jesus told him, "Go home to your own people, and report to them how much the Lord has done for you and how he has had mercy on you" (Mark 5:19). Because of this man, an entire region named Decapolis heard the good news. He was once in bondage to the evil one but now is liberated by the mercy of Jesus. Mark records how his village responded to Jesus and I believe it was a result of his witness (Mark 6:53–56). This man was set free to be commissioned to work in the harvest fields. How much different would the world be if every believer obeyed this command?

Neither the slave girl or the man possessed by a demon may seem like strong candidates for people of peace. Yet God used the "impossible cases" as a testimony of his power. Nothing awakens an entire town quite like the testimony of deliverance from a former demoniac, addict, and abuser. Do not be guilty of writing someone off as too hard or too calloused for the gospel message. Truly no one is too far gone for the power of God. Continue to pray and engage people because God specializes in the hard cases.

Spiritual Receptivity Maximizes Opportunities—the Good and the Bad

God intervenes in all types of circumstances to create and maximize spiritual receptivity. Desperate people (or tired people or confused people or hurt people) make good soil for the gospel. Surprisingly, excited people—those who are experiencing positive life transitions, such as a new job or marriage or the birth of a baby—also make good soil for the gospel. Think about the scene in Philippi where Paul and Silas were chained in prison. The jailer may have been one of the men who actually beat them. He may have looked on in amazement as they suffered the torture with grace. Likely he witnessed them singing songs of worship and heard their prayers, enduring suffering for Christ's sake. After the earthquake released the prisoner's chains, God had the jailer's full attention. On the verge of taking his own life, he heard the voice of Paul: "'Don't harm yourself, because we're all here!'" (Acts 16:28). In a twist of divine irony, the jailer called for a light. Little did he know that the Light of the world would soon enter the darkness of his heart. The Lord opened the jailer's heart to the gospel as he asked, "What must I do to be saved?" Ever wondered how it occurred to the jailer to ask to be saved? One can only speculate, but clearly the jailer paid attention to Paul and Silas's faith, and when his heart was open, the Holy Spirit intervened.

The story of the jailer's conversion instructs us on where and how to find persons of peace: it's likely going to happen in the middle of opposition and in the face of apparent defeat. God allows difficult circumstances because he has a greater purpose in mind. Bible characters such as Joseph, Job, and Daniel would all attest to this truth. Paul would later write to these same Philippians about how his being in jail in Rome happened for the furtherance of the gospel (Phil 1:12). The secret confidence every believer can attest to is knowing all things will work together for good because they love God and are called according to his purpose (Rom 8:28). Now, that's divine synergy! We as believers can look in places of pain and know that the "for good" might be the salvation of this person and an entire relational network.

God also shows us in this story what to do when we encounter a person of peace: we respectfully listen to their questions and let them talk. They may very well be asking us for the reason of the hope within us (1 Pet 3:15). It's also important to remember to get to the gospel. Some people dance around the gospel, spending all their time developing relationships. But receptive people must hear the truth of the Word of God at the right time. There is only one relationship that will secure their eternity in heaven. It's the one relationship that they must have and that's with Jesus.

In addition to listening and sharing the gospel, we also need to follow up with discipleship and helping them evangelize their relational networks (Acts 16:32–40). Be vulnerable and open to the people God providentially puts in your path. The Holy Spirit is opportunistic and completely able to open hearts to the gospel. Do not fear rejection because the gospel has the dynamic to change lives. If they reject you it's truly a rejection of Jesus Christ (Luke 10:16).

Spiritual Receptivity Expressed in the Twenty-First Century

People of peace are all around us. Mission Arlington in Texas, anchored within First Baptist Church, has built an effective multifamily housing ministry and experienced a localized church planting movement by looking for spiritual receptivity. Multifamily housing communities—largely apartment communities and mobile home parks—are often overlooked and ignored in large and small cities alike. Yet this is exactly where Mission Arlington focuses because these communities are often very open and receptive to ministry.

Over thirty years ago, Tillie Burgin and her family began Mission Arlington. Multi-housing communities have a culture all their own. Apartment dwellers have unique personal experiences (often in crisis or in transition) that open them to the hope of the gospel. It is often a property manager or resident who becomes the first person of peace. Jim Burgin, Tillie's son, passionately shares, "You must hear the cries of the people in the apartments." Effective ministry in a receptive place flows from a burden for the people. Just like in Acts, God has a way of leading us to places with people who are already prepared to hear the gospel. Remember, the first-century church likely did not have a building until the third century. Instead, they often reached people household to household. This is much like God's work in Arlington.[7]

---

[7] Erma H. Mathis, *Mission Arlington: Out to Change the World* (Women's Missionary Union SBC, 2000), 2–3; and personal interviews with Tillie Burgin. For further insight to the ministry of Mission Arlington, see Mission Arlington, http://missionarlington.org/.

Today, Mission Arlington is currently working in over 250 apartments with a huge hub spanning several city blocks to provide various mercy ministries to those in need. Their mission statement speaks volumes of their dependence on spiritual receptivity: "Hang out and hover around John 3:16."

Where are the receptive places within your community? It may be the local coffee shop or YMCA. It could be that participating in a club or special interest group may provide an entrée to share the gospel and open up new relational networks. Perhaps you'll find persons of peace in an ethnic affinity group, restaurant, mosque, or temple. How about connecting with your local school, hospital, nursing home, or social service agency? Remember, people groups cluster together around their ethnic culture, their various affinities, and their unique locations.

The website www.peoplegroups.info is also a great resource. It allows users to carefully examine, naturally encounter, and intentionally engage ethnic linguistic people groups. You can navigate to the tab at the bottom of the home page to "Person of Peace." There you will find excellent biblically-based teachings to help you recognize, discover, and minister to people of peace.

Conclusion

A missionary friend once shared about a person of peace he met and described him this way: "He has the kingdom in his eyes." Can we see people like this? Look around. There are spiritually receptive people both in the biblical stories and in our neighborhood's today:

- A tax collector named Matthew sitting at his table . . . could be someone who works in the public sector.
- A woman of bad reputation drawing water by a well . . . could be a bartender or barista.
- An outcast nameless man of the tombs oppressed by legions of demons . . . could be the poor, addicted, and homeless.

- An Ethiopian eunuch reading Scripture in his chariot . . . could be someone of influence from another country or a refugee.
- A solider named Cornelius seeking to understand a vision . . . could be a veteran or active military soldier or family member.
- A business woman named Lydia seeking God by a river . . . could be a career-oriented business woman.
- A jailer in a suicidal crisis ready to end it all . . . could be the desperate one who lost everything.

These people from Scripture were all waiting for someone to obey the Father and share the hope of the gospel. Gary Mayes, in his book *The DNA of a Revolution*, insightfully writes, "Lots of people are waiting on the other side of our obedience."[8] These modern-day counterparts and their relational networks are all waiting on the other side of our obedience. Let us be faithful to the call.

---

[8] Mayes, *DNA of a Revolution*, 134 (see chap. 2, n. 3).

Acts Immersion

Acts Action Item

Commit to discover and engage persons of peace as you express the DNA of spiritual receptivity in your life and the life of your church.

Culture Change: Experiences and the Missionary Discourses

Jesus taught people how to see, feel, think, and act like a missionary by his lifestyle and through formal times of instruction (Matthew 10; Mark 6:7–13; Luke 10:1–24). If you desire to change the culture of your church, then you need to create experiences that will do so. People learn missions firsthand. The Holy Spirit uses experiences to teach us. Donald McGavran, in his book *Bridges of God*, reminds believers how the teams in Acts intentionally sought-after receptive peoples. He writes:

> As we search for light as to how peoples become Christian, the story of the early church has a great contribution to make. . . . Perhaps most important of all, we saw how the intentional missionary labors of the early church, headed by Paul, were devoted in large measure deliberately to following responsive peoples and to expanding existing impulses to Christ in the hearts of people.[9]

It's practice, not theory, that makes the difference in discovering persons of peace. Be sure to complete the missionary activities at the conclusion of each chapter. It's in those field experiences where the real learning occurs.

---

[9] Donald McGavran, *Bridges of God: A Study in the Strategy of Missions* (Eugene, OR: Wipf and Stock, 1950), 35.

Acts Character and Competence

Be . . .

- prayerful—keep prayer at the forefront of all mission activity
- relational—learn to meet new people and listen to God's voice
- opportunistic—discovering those persons of peace in your mission field

Know . . .

- that a person of peace can maximize gospel impact through their household (relational network)
- that God uses opportunities and circumstances (good or bad) to discover persons of peace
- that God is able to set anyone free, do not write off anyone as they may be spiritual receptive

Do . . .

- Prayerfully read the daily devotional "Acts Moment" and the Acts Bible readings.
- Map the constellation of your relationships (family, friends, neighbors, associations, etc.).
- Seek to discover and engage a person of peace from your relationship map.
- Pray for a person who seems to be hopeless and unreceptive.
- Ask God to fill you with his Holy Spirit afresh and anew to be his witness.
- Commit to utilize the *ACTS Prayer Guide* at the weekly corporate prayer or your personal prayer time.

Acts Reading

Day 1: Acts 10:23-48
Day 2: Acts 11:1-18
Day 3: Acts 11:19-30
Day 4: Acts 12:1-19
Day 5: Acts 12:20-25

Acts Missionary Activity

Spiritual Receptivity: Discover a Person of Peace and Their Network

This week take some time to speak with an unreached person or new believer in your community who you have been praying for. Share with them what you have learned about the reach and potential of their networks of relationships. Start with your own constellation of relationships: family, friends, neighbors, and associates. Map these out on a piece of paper. Then explore with them who is in their relational network. Ask questions about their networks and be sure to thank them for helping you learn. (Remember to focus on family, friends, neighbors, and associates.) In your personal prayer time, intercede for the people you and they identified on your map.

Reflection: What did you discover about this person's spiritual receptivity and their relational network?

Spiritual Receptivity in the Life of Christ

Jesus modeled the strategic person of peace DNA principle through discovering and engaging receptive people.

For Further Reading

- *Organic Church* by Neil Cole
- *Tradecraft* by Larry E. McCrary
- *Miraculous Movements* by Jerry Truesdale

7

Spiritual Sowing: Evangelize and Make Disciples
(Thessalonica/Berea)

Those who sow in tears will reap with shouts of joy. Though one goes along weeping, carrying the bag of seed, he will surely come back with shouts of joy, carrying his sheaves.
—Psalms 126:5–6

Christian disciples are sent, men and women—sent out in the same work and world evangelism to which the Lord was sent, and for which He gave His life. Evangelism is not an optional accessory to our life. It is the heartbeat of all that we are called to be and do.
—Robert Coleman, *The Master Plan of Evangelism*

John Chapman was born on September 26, 1774 in Leominster, Massachusetts. A nurseryman by trade, he could often be found planting trees in his village or setting up another orchard on a plot of land. A little eccentric, Chapman wore a weathered seed sack with holes cut out for his head and arms. He had a full beard and sported a tin bowl of a hat that resembled a cooking pot. Traveling barefoot, he moved beyond his village to plant trees in other states and even Canada.

The pioneer people loved him deeply because he would trade with them for trees, providing fruit for their survival. He was particularly partial to the apple tree, which he introduced everywhere he went. Made from the stuff of legends—you might know him better by his nickname, Johnny Appleseed.[1] He died in March of 1845 in Fort Wayne, Indiana.

Genetic research has greatly influenced how farmers raise crops. Fruits such as apples can now be made disease-resistant and produced in new, more flavorful varieties. Despite the innovations in farming technology, however, the simple practices of planting the seed, nurturing the seedling, or grafting for new growth is still the same as it was for Johnny Appleseed. The same is true for the church today. Despite the incredible technological advancements in the world, the twenty-first century church has the same Holy Spirit, the same Word of God, the same gospel message, and the same opportunities the early church did. In fact, it's likely this generation has even greater opportunities than the first-century church did through things like technology and ease of travel.

Jesus spoke of sowing Johnny-Appleseed style: "'The kingdom of God is like this,' he said. 'A man scatters seed on the ground. He sleeps and rises night and day; the seed sprouts and grows, although he doesn't know how'" (Mark 4:26–27). The sower doesn't know how the seed sprouts and grows, but he stays at the task. Beyond what we can see and know, God is mysteriously at work in both plants and the hearts of lost people, desiring to produce a sprouting crop of new converts and growing disciples. Johnny Appleseed wasn't thinking about growing one apple or even several bushels of apples. He was thinking grand orchards for all-out production that outlived him. Author Christian Schwarz writes, "The fruit of the apple tree is

---

[1] Howard Means, *Johnny Appleseed: The Man, the Myth, the American Story* (New York: Simon and Schuster, 2011), 3–7. See also Biography.com Editors, "Johnny Appleseed," Biography, https://www.biography.com/people/johnny-appleseed-38103.

not an apple . . . it is an orchard."² What do you and your church see when looking at the harvest—an apple on one tree, bushels of apples, or orchards filled with truckloads of apples?

The Purpose of Spiritual Sowing

The next strand of DNA in the book of Acts is *spiritual sowing* and its application naturally moves us toward an orchard mentality. We express spiritual sowing in a commitment to evangelize the lost and make disciples for Christ. These missional actions might be best understood as two sides of the same coin. One side is evangelizing and the other is making disciples. If you and your church practice healthy evangelism then there ought to be healthy discipleship present and vice versa.

Spiritual sowing was Jesus's priority (Matt 4:17). He intentionally looked for opportunities to sow. Even his own sacrificial death, burial, and resurrection was and is a testament to spiritual sowing as the seed of his own life was sown—falling to the ground to die and then to rise again, producing much fruit. Jesus said, "Truly I tell you, unless a grain of wheat falls to the ground and dies, it remains by itself. But if it dies, it produces much fruit" (John 12:24). The heart of the gospel was exhibited in his love and compassion for lost humanity—spiritual sowing is about sacrifice and multiplication. God asks that we be about his agenda. In the midst of our busy schedules and church budgets and corporate goals, God asks us to be interruptable. Will we follow God at any moment to sow into his kingdom? Will we give anything he asks of us? Kingdom multiplication and production are only attained by dying to ourselves for the sake of lost humanity.

We can see healthy examples of spiritual sowing in how the churches in Thessalonica and Berea began (Acts 17:1–15). As was his pattern, Paul went to the Jewish synagogue in Thessalonica and reasoned with them from Scripture. Some among them believed and joined Paul. But in a familiar

---

² Christian Schwarz, *Color Your World with Natural Church Development* (Saint Charles, IL: ChurchSmart, 2005), 95.

chorus, some of the other Jews became jealous and incited a riot in the city. They accused Paul and Barnabas of "turn[ing] the world upside down" (vv. 2–6). This is exactly what spiritual sowing does: it turns worlds upside down. Actually, from God's vantage point, Thessalonica-style sowing turns the world right side up, stirring things up for God's kingdom purpose (Acts 17:6). Henry Blackaby emphatically writes:

> If Christians around the world were to suddenly renounce their personal agendas, their life goals and their aspirations, and begin responding in radical obedience to everything God showed them, the world would be turned upside down. How do we know? Because that's what first century Christians did, and the world is still talking about it.[3]

It all begins with a love relationship with Jesus Christ and is driven by radical obedience to God. Evangelism and disciple making were not *a* ministry of the first-century church; it was *the* ministry of the church.[4] Without spiritual sowing, the church is intentionally disobedient to Jesus's final command, and the next generation stands to be lost.

The great need of the day is for gospel intentionality. Spiritual sowing may be the most suppressed principle of the church today—and possibly the one most under attack by the devil. The subtle shift in most churches is to major on minor things in comparison to winning lost souls. The devil has distracted most believers from the main thing and provoked a divorce of evangelism from discipleship and discipleship from evangelism. This is nothing short of a genetic mutation.

Yet the proverbial apple doesn't fall far from the tree. When you follow Jesus, you will evangelize and make disciples—and by ripple effect influence

---

[3] Henry Blackaby and Richard Blackaby, *Spiritual Leadership: Moving People on to God's Agenda* (Nashville: B&H, 2011), 29.

[4] Jeff Christopherson of Send Network has shared the distinction between churches started *for* evangelism and churches started *from* evangelism in Christopherson and Lake, *Kingdom First*, 2 (see chap. 2, n. 4).

those around you to do the same. Charles Spurgeon said, "Soul-winning is the chief business of the Christian minister; indeed, it should be the main pursuit of every true believer."[5] Ask yourself the question: Is winning souls my chief pursuit? Jesus said, "Follow me, and I will make you fish for people" (Matt 4:19). It makes sense—those who follow Jesus fish for men and women and children. Soul winners win souls. Witnesses bear witness. Evangelists evangelize. Shepherds search for lost sheep. Disciples make disciples. Sowing leads to reaping.

Spiritual Sowing Produces a Response

When Paul and Silas entered Thessalonica, they possessed a complete confidence in the gospel message and an equal confidence in God. The gospel was sown into the hearts of the people; first in the synagogue and then to the Greeks along with the leading women of the city. They found a mix of both good soil and bad soil. At the synagogue, they discovered Jason—a person of peace—which lead to more spiritual sowing within the whole city (Acts 17:1–2; 7). Preston Parrish said, "The Gospel is a living seed. When this message is proclaimed and sown into hearts and lives, God blesses it as he blesses no other message. The seed of the gospel bears fruit in the form of changed lives."[6] This takes the pressure off the messenger and shifts the dependence on the Holy Spirit's power through God's message.

God turned everything right side up, causing all kinds of trouble for the status quo in Thessalonica, but from the world's perspective the world was turned upside down. Have you ever thought about the fact that riots and revivals often go hand in hand? The gospel always produces a response: sometimes it changes lives and sometimes it threatens the status quo. Paul

---

[5] Charles H. Spurgeon, *The Soul Winner: How to Lead Sinners to the Savior* (Grand Rapids: Eerdmans, 1963), 322.

[6] Joy Allmond, "Sowing the Seeds of the Gospel around the World," Billy Graham Evangelistic Association website, January 4, 2001, https://billygraham.org/story/sowing-the-seeds-of-the-gospel-around-the-world/.

and his team were called disturbers (Acts 17:6). If you sow the gospel, then you can count on turning the world upside down for the sake of God's kingdom advance.

The villages of Thessalonica and Berea received the gospel very differently. Initially, there were a number of people in Thessalonica who rejected Christ. The missionary team had to leave town under the cover of darkness. But in Berea there was great receptivity. Many "noble" Jews eagerly examined the word daily and welcomed the gospel (vv. 10–12). The gospel seed had been planted in good soil where it sprouted and grew, producing fruit. There is, incidentally, no record of rejection in Berea.

Notice the difference in attitude between the Thessalonians and the Bereans toward Scripture. Commentator John Stott writes:

> Yet one important aspect of them, to which he seems to be drawing his readers' attention, is the attitude to the Scriptures adopted by both speaker and hearers, as evidenced by the verbs he uses. In Thessalonica Paul reasoned, explained, proved, proclaimed and persuaded, while in Berea the Jews eagerly received the message and diligently examined the Scriptures.[7]

The preaching in Acts is consistently about the cross, resurrection, and exaltation of Jesus. But *how* the message is conveyed changes. In the account of the work at the Thessalonica synagogue, Luke uses five words for spiritual sowing: *reasoning, explaining, proving, proclaiming,* and *persuading*. Each word describes a different approach we can use to share the gospel and make disciples. We'll look at each one in turn.

Spiritually Sowing through Reasoning

God has called us, just like he did Paul and Silas, to rationally present the truth. Reason demonstrates the ability to use logic and positive argument

---

[7] John W. Stott, *The Spirit, the Church and the World* (Downers Grove, IL: Intervarsity Press, 1994), 274.

to make the case for Christ (Acts 17:2). The challenge is to defend the faith that was once delivered to us and at the same time readily share the reason for our hope in Christ (Jude 3; 1 Pet 3:15). This scriptural apologetic began in the synagogue and moved out into the streets.

The Greek word *dielexato* conveys "thinking different things with oneself" captured by first pondering and then disputing with others.[8] The dialogue wasn't one way but a two-way conversation that Paul had with Jews based on Scripture. Likewise, in Athens, he first pondered the best line of reasoning with those philosophers and then respectfully disputed with them.

A person does not have to void his or her intelligence and ability to reason when sharing, or even considering, the claims of the gospel. As a matter of trust, your assignment is to humbly reason with them, always giving God the elbow room to work. For the thoughtful disputer, there are many helpful resources available to use and two of the best examples are C. S. Lewis's *Mere Christianity* and Lee Strobel's *The Case for Christ*. Always remember, though, that when reasoning with an unbeliever the greatest resource is still the Holy Spirit and the Word of God.

Spiritually Sowing through Explaining

God has called you, just like he did Paul and Silas, to sow the truth with clarity. This word translated "explain" is found in the account of Paul's interaction with the Jews in Thessalonica (Acts 17:3). This word quickly takes us back to Acts 8:30–31 where Philip the evangelist shared the gospel with the Ethiopian who inquired, "How can I understand, unless someone guides me?" People who are sincerely seeking need a guide to explain the meaning of the gospel message. The Greek word *(dianoigon)* is used to describe the opening of a blind man's eyes with the outcome of opening completely.[9]

---

[8] W. E. Vine, *An Expository Dictionary of New Testament Words: With Their Precise Meanings for English Readers* (Iowa Falls, IA: Riverside Book and Bible House, 1952), 924.

[9] Vine, 813.

The prefix is *dia*, which means "through." A person who encounters the gospel must have a breakthrough to see and recognize how the light of God's truth applies to their dark, sinful condition. Paul and Silas were more than ready to explain, trusting God to illuminate to the Jews that Jesus is the Messiah who fulfilled the prophecies of the Old Testament.

People have many misconceptions and false assumptions about spiritual things. The tendency among many believers is to make the simple complex. A major part of your God-given assignment is to help move unbelievers closer toward the gospel. The decision to accept Christ doesn't necessarily happen overnight, though it certainly can. An excellent tool called the Engel Scale can be used to measure and track how near or far someone may be to crossing the line to receiving Christ.[10] There is a general pattern many follow as they come to believe in Christ. Explaining the gospel can be as simple as bringing a person one step closer to the point of salvation. Dennis Pethers defines evangelism as "leaving a person I met with a better understanding of God than they would have had if they'd never met me."[11] The Holy Spirit will guide you to authentically explain God's truth in such a way that it can be comprehended and grasped either on the spot or at a later time.

Spiritually Sowing through Proving

God has called you, just as he did Paul and Silas, to sow and confirm the truth of the gospel. The Greek word translated "prove" *(paratithemenos)* contains the prefix *para*, meaning to lay alongside a known truth (consistent with the word *parable*). It means to allege, commend, or entrust by way of argument.[12] The Berean sister church eagerly examined the Scriptures every day to see (or prove) that what was said was truth. Luke began the book of

---

[10] James Engel and William Dyrness, *Changing the Mind of Missions: Where Have We Gone Wrong?* (Downers Grove: IL: InterVarsity, 2000).

[11] Quoted in Polly House, "Small Groups Key to Spiritual Growth," Baptist Press, August 16, 2010, http://www.bpnews.net/33525.

[12] Vine, *An Expository Dictionary of New Testament Words*, 39.

Acts with what he called the "many proofs" that all pointed to the fact Jesus Christ is who he said he was (Acts 1:3). The most important elements in proving the validity of the gospel message is in presenting the preponderance of evidence and living out the life of Christ before the people.

In Thessalonica, a good example of living proof is how Jason paid a considerable personal price—both physical assault and financial loss—for his willingness to follow Christ. The implication of Jason's house coming to faith in Jesus emphasizes the combination of the closely related strands of DNA—spiritual receptivity and spiritual sowing (Acts 17:5–9). The persecuted believers in the first century were described as proven witnesses. John wrote about those believers in Revelation, "They conquered him [the devil] by the blood of the Lamb and by the word of their testimony; they did not love their lives to the point of death" (Rev 12:11). This witness of faith in action is the meaning behind "prove it"—and for some it meant literally dying for Christ. Each Christ follower proves or misrepresents God's faithful love by their words and deeds.

Spiritually Sowing through Proclaiming

God has called you, just like he did Paul and Silas, to plainly speak the word of the gospel. The Greek word (*katatangello*) is rendered "announce or declare" when translated into English. The word has the nuance "show," such as in Paul's teaching about the Lord's Supper, which proclaims or "shows" his death till he comes (1 Cor 11:26). It is a picture sermon.[13] St. Francis of Assisi said, "Preach the gospel at all times and when necessary use words."[14] This is well and good in a society where everyone is preaching something with words, but we can't forget there must be an actual speaking of the

---

[13] Vine, 1237.

[14] Mark Galli, "Speak the Gospel: Use Deeds If Necessary" (an article on the discussion of the origin of the quote attributed to St. Francis), *Christianity Today*, May 21, 2009, http://www.christianitytoday.com/ct/2009/mayweb-only/120-42.0.html?share=jP7aE4SVSEUdVEn29h44VOGnsw0pS1BY.

gospel. J. D. Greear states, "With all due respect for St. Francis, how can you preach the gospel of Christ's finished work without words? That's like saying, 'Tell me your phone number. If necessary, use digits.' The announcement consists of words."[15] There is something wrong when the church goes silent thinking if we live a good life before the lost that will be enough. The gospel is both show *and* tell. Yes, our life must match our message. That is indisputable. But we must remember, "Faith comes from what is heard, and what is heard comes through the message of Christ" (Rom 10:17).

F. F. Bruce writes, "The book of Acts tells us that many wonders and signs were done by the apostles (Acts 2:43), but the book of Acts emphasizes preaching as a major tool of evangelism (Acts 2:32; 3:15; 5:32; 10:39; 13:31; 22:15)."[16] The gospel proclamation is more involved than just a simple declaration. The preaching of the cross always calls for a decision and response. Proclaiming the gospel of Jesus includes both declaration and invitation. Here are two sobering thoughts from Paul with grave implications related to sowing the word through proclamation:

1. "The message of the cross is foolishness to those who are perishing" (1 Cor 1:18).
2. "Woe is me, if I preach not the gospel" (1 Cor 9:16).

How is your passion and seriousness for proclamation?

Spiritually Sowing through Persuading

God has called you, just like he did Paul and Silas, to persuade people to come to Christ. The root of the Greek word *epeisthesan* is "believe," which is most commonly translated "were persuaded" and even hints at obedience.[17] The word *persuade* may cause concern because it can stir up images

---

[15] J. D. Greear, *Jesus Continued: Why the Spirit Inside You Is Better than Jesus Beside You* (Grand Rapids: Zondervan, 2014), 57.

[16] Bruce, *New International Commentary: Acts*, 38–39 (see chap. 4, n. 7).

[17] Vine, *An Expository Dictionary of New Testament Words*, 888.

of manipulation and arm twisting. The truth of the matter is that if you could talk someone into becoming a Christian then someone could just as easily talk them out of it. Our job is to persuade. It is left to the Holy Spirit to convict.

Persuasion is a good thing. We see in Acts 26 that Paul eloquently attempts to persuade King Agrippa to believe, and again in Acts 28 Paul tries to persuade the Jews to believe in Jesus before declaring that the salvation of God is going to the Gentiles because "they will listen" (v. 28). Just as in Paul's day, people today are in danger of eternal judgment. The fear of the Lord motivates us to evangelize and make disciples. Paul said, "Therefore, since we know the fear of the Lord, we try to persuade people. What we are is plain to God, and I hope it is also plain to your consciences" (2 Cor 5:11). Far from being a tool of manipulation, biblical persuasion is always flowing from the love of Christ (2 Cor 5:14).

Spiritual sowing can be a gratifying part of the missional rhythm and flow of your life. Each of us must make evangelism and discipleship a daily decision. The natural tendency is to drift from the practice. Evangelism is simply being present to introduce a person to Jesus Christ. It can be compared to a midwife in the birthing process. Evangelism occurs when a person is lovingly confronted to respond by saying yes or no to the truth of the gospel (1 Thess 1:9). Discipleship is nurturing a person to the point of new birth and continuing like a mother to watch her precious children grow in Christ-likeness (1 Thess 2:4–8). Like in Acts, when these five approaches to spiritual sowing occur, the number of new disciples and churches exponentially multiplies.

Spiritual Sowing Produces New Churches

Kevin Ezell, president of the North American Mission Board, insightfully notes that "Gospel conversations lead to gospel congregations."[18] Likewise,

---

[18] Mike Ebert, "Ezell: SBC needs a 'Gospel Conversation Resurgence'," Baptist Press, June 15, 2017, http://www.bpnews.net/49065/ezell-sbc-needs-a-gospel-conversation-resurgence.

the often-quoted line from missiologist C. Peter Wagner reminds the church, "Church planting is the single most effective evangelistic methodology under heaven."[19] The sowing of the gospel was central to church planting in Acts because authentic church planting was and has always been about evangelizing and making disciples. Spiritual sowing not only produces a response, it also leads to new churches. Real Life Church in Post Falls, Idaho, is a beautiful example. The church began with four families in 1998 and now averages over 8,500 in worship. Their mission is to "reach the world for Jesus one person at a time." Pastor Jim Putman has a heartbeat for intentional spiritual sowing, believing that "Christianity is like the flu—it's caught person-to-person."[20] He believes each church needs to establish a system through which the lost are reached for Christ and disciples are made. Their desire at Real Life Church is to take the accidental out of evangelism and discipleship. He writes:

> At Real Life Ministries, our overriding goal is to train disciples who know how to disciple others. In our church, everyday Christians do the work of disciple making and fill the majority of our staff positions. We are able to reach the lost in our area because everyone in our congregation plays a part in the church's mission.[21]

Real Life Church has started over six churches and has truly turned their part of the world upside down through sharing the gospel one person at a time.

---

[19] C. Peter Wagner, *Church Planting for a Greater Harvest: A Comprehensive Guide* (Ventura, CA: Regal Books), 11.

[20] Jim Putman, *Real Life Discipleship*, Heartland Church Network, accessed July 21, 2013, http://www.heartlandchurchnetwork.com/uploads/5/8/1/6/581 63279/real_life_discipleship_1.pdf.

[21] Jim Putman, *Real Life Discipleship* (n.p.: Tyndale House, 2014), introduction. For more information and to hear messages, see the Real Life Church website at https://www.reallifechurch.org/.

Conclusion

The book of Acts shows us over and over that the result of spiritual sowing is more new believers, more disciples, and more new churches. The church at Jerusalem experienced daily additions of new believers (Acts 2:40). Could it be the reason the average church is not experiencing daily additions is because the average member is not sharing the gospel every day? Those believers scattered by the persecution headed to Antioch, organically carrying the gospel to all those they encountered, and the message went viral (Acts 11:19–21). Imagine if every believer in every church in North America determined to share the gospel daily. The result could be daily additions to the church, whole communities transformed with God's glory, and an abundance of new churches planted.

I have a small plaque in my office that serves as a daily reminder of the multiplication link between evangelism and church planting. It says, "Anyone can count the seeds in an apple, but only God can count the number of apples in a seed." Are we thinking orchards or a single tree? Spiritual sowing is our priority. It is the result of the overflow of our walk with Christ. Now is the time and there is a harvest of souls to be reaped by everyday Christ followers who are living on mission.

Join me in this beautiful prayer:

> God, give me an OPPORTUNITY today to speak to someone about Christ;
> Give me WISDOM to see it;
> Give me the BOLDNESS to seize it.[22]

With abundant sowing, an abundant harvest awaits us!

---

[22] Alvin Reid, *Sharing Jesus without Freaking Out: Evangelism the Way You Were Born to Do It* (Nashville: B&H, 2017), 18. See also the Gospel Life website: http://www.gospel-life.net/sharing-christ-every-single-day-a-threefold-prayer/.

Acts Immersion

Acts Action Item

Commit to intentionally evangelize by sharing the gospel and making disciples in your life and the life of your church.

Culture Change: Missional Preaching and Hearing the Word

God can use the preaching of the book of Acts to change the missional culture of a church. Consider Moses, who gave an excuse that he could not speak. Since stuttering generally runs in the family, scientists have long suspected there is a genetic variant that might lead to this particular speech impediment.

> In 2010, researchers with the National Institutes of Health (NIH) have identified three genes that may predispose people to stuttering—a condition that affects 3 million Americans and 5% of young children.[23]

There is a hope that treatments and early detection may help people address this from a positive perspective. When Moses stood amazed before God at the burning bush, God called him to be a deliverer for the children of Israel. Moses said that he could not speak, which meant that Aaron would become his mouthpiece (Exod 3).

In reality, there is not one preacher alive who can lay claim to having any ability to speak for God (all of us are slow of speech and stutter!). Al Tizon, in his book *Missional Preaching*, writes, "Kingdom-shaped, missional preaching does its indispensable part in molding the people of God to be

---

[23] Salynn Boyles, "Genetic Mutations Linked to Stuttering: Researchers Identify Three Genes That May Play a Role in Stuttering," WebMD, February 10, 2010, https://www.webmd.com/children/news/20100210/genetic-mutations-linked-to-stuttering#1.

the city on a hill, the salt of the earth and the light of the world."[24] Listen intently to the book of Acts. God is at work sowing a missional message for us to believe and put into practice.

Acts Character and Competence

Be...

- intentional—seek opportunities to sow the gospel from every angle
- partnership-oriented—realizing some people sow, some water, but God gives the increase
- faithful—to the gospel message, preaching the truth of the cross and resurrection

Know...

- that spiritual sowing is planting gospel seeds in good and bad soil
- that God gives the increase in the harvest; our responsibility is to sow and water (1 Cor 3:6)
- that abundantly sowing the gospel is essential to advancing the kingdom and planting a new church

Do...

- Prayerfully read the daily devotional "Acts Moment" and the Acts Bible readings below.
- Identify a person to share the gospel with and to disciple for Christ.
- Share the gospel with that person this week and teach them how to walk with Christ.
- Pray for the lost people by name.
- Ask God to fill you with his Holy Spirit afresh and anew to be his witness.

---

[24] Al Tizon, *Missional Preaching: Engage Embrace Transform* (Valley Forge, PA: Judson Press, 2012), 17.

- Commit to utilize the *ACTS Prayer Guide* at the weekly corporate prayer or your personal prayer time.

Acts Reading

Day 1: Acts 13:1–3
Day 2: Acts 13:4–12
Day 3: Acts 13:13–52
Day 4: Acts 14:1–20
Day 5: Acts 14:21–28

Acts Missionary Activity

Spiritual Sowing: Scripture Distribution

This week, plan to go either to a neighbor, a waitress, or even a stranger with a small New Testament in hand to give as a gift. Pray before, during, and after your encounter with this person. Believe the promise, "So the word that comes from my mouth will not return to me empty, but will accomplish what I please and will prosper in what I send it to do" (Isa 55:11). Thank God for the privilege and a good first missional step of sowing the gospel through Bible distribution.

Reflection: How did it feel to sow the gospel through giving a Bible?

Spiritual Sowing in the Life of Christ

Jesus modeled the spiritual DNA of sowing as he communicated the good news with the lost and naturally made disciples.

For Further Reading

- *The Master Plan of Evangelism* by Robert Coleman
- *Share Jesus Without Fear* by Bill Faye
- *Real-Life Discipleship Training* by Jim Putman

8

Spiritual Bridges: Leverage Points of Connection
(Athens)

For as I was passing through and observing the objects of your worship, I even found an altar on which was inscribed: TO AN UNKNOWN GOD. Therefore, what you worship in ignorance, this I proclaim to you.
—Acts 17:23

If our churches are to remain relevant to our culture, then they must spend time exegeting that culture as well as the Scriptures. . . . Not only must we know how to exegete the Bible; we must be able to exegete the culture in which we live.
—Aubrey Malphurs, *Planting Growing Churches for the Twenty-First Century*

There are all kinds of bridges around the world. More than likely, the first bridge was just a tree that fell over a creek and allowed people to cross to the other side.[1] There is a little-known bridge in Singapore called the Helix Bridge. It is a pedestrian bridge spanning over 900 feet, linking Marina Centre with Marina South. Interestingly, the bridge is designed as a double helix (DNA) structure, representing rebirth and growth for the city and its people.[2] As all bridges, it's designed to span a divide and provide passage over a gap or barrier—to get you between the "here" and the "there."

The next DNA principle is *spiritual bridges* exemplified by Paul's efforts on Mars Hill in Athens (Acts 17:15–34). Paul inevitably crossed many bridges on his missionary journeys throughout Asia Minor. Yet in Athens, God used him to teach future believers and churches how to bridge the gap for the sake of the gospel.

The Purpose of Spiritual Bridges

Every believer is called to find common ground with lost people to share the hope of the gospel with them. This is the art of spiritual bridges. The gospel message does not change although the approach and the method must change as the context does. Consider the differences in how Paul preaches to the Jews in Acts 13:16–41 and the Lycaonian Gentiles in Acts 14:8–18. To the Jews he references Israelite history and the law of Moses. To the Lycaonians he references world history and the natural law. Jesus Christ is proclaimed to both groups but the bridge to his listeners is different. Spiritual bridges move a person from being *here*—lost without Christ—to *there*—receiving the gift of eternal life in Christ and becoming his disciple.

Bridge-building is simple but too often fear stops us from sharing the gospel. There are some believers who suffer spiritually from gephyrophobia: the fear of crossing bridges. Sometimes we'll drive a different route to avoid

---

[1] K. Waule, "The Bridge as a Test of Civilization," *Scientific American Quarterly* (March 1921): 201.

[2] Alaric Anderson, "Top Ten Most Awesome and Unusual Bridges That You Can Hardly Believe Actually Exist," *Tech Reader*, June 14, 2016, https://thetechreader.com/top-ten/top-ten-most-awesome-and-unusual-bridges-that-you-can-hardly-believe-actually-exist/.

the bridge—and the rejection, pain, or embarrassment it might cause. But remember Paul's words: "To the weak, I became weak, in order to win the weak. I have become all things to all people, so that I may by every possible means save some. Now I do all this because of the gospel, so that I may share in the blessings" (2 Cor 9:22–23). This was Paul's guiding principle in building spiritual bridges and it can be ours.

In addition to fear, bridge building is thwarted when we fail to walk wisely in the world but not be of the world. Missiologist Ed Stetzer writes:

> The gospel never fits properly within a culture. Two parallel problems keep many believers from truly engaging the unchurched culture. Christians tend to love or despise the culture too much.[3]

This modern genetic mutation lives in one of two extremes. It's either embracing a culture so deeply there is no distinguishing marks of holiness remaining in us. Or, it's an outright refusal to engage lost people, despising individuals or culture so much we're detached from those God has called us to reach. In order to avoid these extremes, our task is to stay within the guardrails of "biblically faithful" and "culturally appropriate" just as Paul and his team did.[4] God has established the Scriptures as his plumbline to use when constructing spiritual bridges. This is what it means to be biblically faithful. Likewise, Jesus embodied appropriate cultural interaction best illustrated by his ability to be a friend to sinners and not a friend of sin. Jesus mastered this balance between the two extremes and his disciples in Acts did as well.

---

[3] R. Stanton Norman, Ed Stetzer, and Daniel Akin, *The Mission of Today's Church: Baptist Leaders Look at Modern Faith Issues* (Nashville: B&H, 2007), 152.

[4] Keelan Cook, "Biblically Faithful or Culturally Relevant: Why Not Both?" *The Peoples Next Door* (blog), September 26, 2016, http://blog.keelancook.com/2016/09/biblically-faithful-or-culturally-relevant-why-not-both.html.

How to Build a Spiritual Bridge

The practice of spiritual bridge building begins with a burden in your heart for the lost. Paul was in Athens waiting for Timothy and Silas to return. While he was waiting, God was working in his heart and among the people of the city (Acts 17:14–16). Paul was "deeply distressed" when he observed the city completely given over to idolatry. Luke described his feelings with the Greek word *paroxysm*, meaning "sharpen" as well as "storm." The word implies an outburst or spasm (Acts 17:16).[5] He felt an intense sharpness burst within him and was compelled to speak up. Paul knew the idols of Athens were worthless and lifeless substitutes for the one true living God.

The longer Paul observed the activities of the Athenians, the more troubled he became. He couldn't wait for the rest of the team and acted with Holy Spirit-led urgency. It was a bridge-over-troubled-water moment for him. How about us? Are we troubled by the lostness in our cities? When we observe people turning to idols and rejecting the living God, do our hearts twinge with pain, compelling us to speak? It truly does begin with a burden for the lost. If you don't feel a burden for the lost, ask God to give you his love for his lost sheep.

The next step in effective bridge building is to address our thinking. We have to seek the mind of Christ as we contextualize our message. For Paul, this contextualization process began with an *exegesis* (a serious interpretation or explanation) of the culture in each city. By way of example, a faithful and diligent student of the Bible exegetes the text to understand the grammar, word meanings, background settings, culture nuances, and how it compares to other passages. We must become students of the culture and the people we're called to reach—both finding common ground and removing as many barriers as possible.

Through observation, Paul found several points of connection with his audience. Paul quickly grabbed onto their idol dedicated to the "unknown

---

[5] Vine, *An Expository Dictionary of New Testament Words*, 900 (see chap. 7, n. 8).

god" as a bridge. He also created bridges around the wonder of creation and the beauty of contemporary poetry. Author Darrell Bock states, "Paul knows his own message and the mentality of the people he evangelizes."[6] How well do we know the message and the mentality of the people God is calling us to reach?

There are many ways for you and me to connect with unbelievers today. We'll look at them briefly together.

The Bridge of Religion

Paul began his time in Athens in the Jewish synagogue. His common ground was their Jewish heritage and the Hebrew Scriptures. An example of a religious bridge for us today is the many Muslims who have been drawn to Christ through visions, as well as those who have been won to him by the Camel method using parts of the Koran (Gospels and Old Testament books) to share the gospel.[7] God is at work to set people free from religious systems that enslave people and provide no hope.

The Bridge of Philosophy

Everyone has some sort of philosophy of life or worldview—the lenses or filters from which they see and respond to the things of God. This may be where you need to build a bridge when encountering those who do not know they need to know God. In Acts there were the Epicureans who were devoted to food, drink, and amusement and the Stoics who strove to muster inner strength, fortitude, and self-control. Today there are those caught up in chasing the American dream and those living in constant fear for what awful thing will happen next. The philosophy of hedonism is prominent, manifested by the pursuit of worldly pleasures. In contrast, moralism runs a

---

[6] Darrell L. Bock, *Acts* (Grand Rapids: Baker Book House, 2007), 573.

[7] Kevin Greeson, *The Camel Method: How Muslims Are Coming to Faith in Christ* (Monument, CO: WIGTake Resources, 2010), 2–9.

close second in modern culture and has proven to be a futile attempt to be good apart from God's grace and mercy in Christ. Once you identify a person's worldview, like Paul, you can find common ground for bridge building.

The Bridge of Idols

Lost people without Christ will naturally have substitutes for God. Idol worship will always be a part of this world. One of the fascinating things about the people on Mars Hill was that they at least had a God-consciousness and an awareness of their idols. In a *Christianity Today* article, Patrick Mabilog compiled an accurate list of modern idols capturing people's lives: work, success, phones, image, materialism, sex, and money.[8] This list is not exhaustive, but it is enough for us to grasp the truth that any idol or unknown god can become a bridge to the gospel. It could be as simple as connecting the average person's smart phone addiction to connection to God through Jesus Christ. What's important is communicating the lifeless and unfulfilling nature of idolatry and then pointing that person to God.

The Bridge of Creation

When looking up at the immensity of the stars, we see the handiwork of God in the vastness of the universe (Ps 19:1). God created the big things. Then peering through the microscope to see the miniscule DNA molecules we see the handiwork of God at the cellular level (Ps 139:14). God made the little things too. Neil DeGrasse Tyson, astrophysicist, said, "There's as many atoms in a single molecule of your DNA as there are stars in the typical galaxy. We are, each of us, a little Universe."[9] In Athens, Paul begins to

---

[8] Patrick Mabilog, "Putting God First: Five Modern-Day Idols We're in Danger of Letting Take Over Our Lives," *Christianity Today*, April 23, 2016, https://www.christiantoday.com/article/5.modern.day.idols.that.are.taking.over.our.lives/84609.htm.

[9] Neil deGrasse Tyson, *Cosmos: A Spacetime Odyssey* (PBS), episode 2.

share about the God they can know on a personal level and he starts with creation in order to point to a personal God who is the Creator of all (Acts 17:24–29).

Today, the bridge of general revelation is challenging because of the prevalent belief in evolution. Ray Comfort, in his book *How to Know God Exists*, dedicates an entire chapter to make the case for intelligent design through DNA. He reasons that a book requires an author and God is the author of DNA. He writes, "Information requires intelligence, and design requires a designer."[10] Science can become a spiritual bridge to the gospel message as we marvel at God's creation. God's creative activity is part of his nature and creation will always testify of him.

The Bridge of God's Nature

The nature of God is seen in his sufficiency. Paul proclaimed, "Neither is he served by human hands as though he needed anything, since he himself gives everyone life and breath and all things" (Acts 17:25). The sufficiency of the infinite God is a spiritual bridge that puts us in our place and reveals how we are utterly helpless and in desperate need to know God.

God's nature is also revealed in his sovereignty. Paul speaks of how God is in control of a person's nationality, where they live, and their time in history. God orchestrates all things according to his will—Jesus came to this earth in the fullness of time or at just the right time. He is God-incarnate with human genes and born of a virgin (Gal 4:4). The angels declared that Christ is the Lord at his birth. The declaration that Jesus is Lord means he is the boss and absolutely in charge. When we confess Jesus as our Lord from a sincere heart, the declaration affirms that we are submitting to his control over every aspect of our life. For in him we live and move and exist—which is every aspect of life (Acts 17:28). The resurrection is God's exclamation

---

[10] Ray Comfort, *How to Know God Exists: Scientific Proof of God* (Alachua, FL: Bridge-Logos, 2007), 3:33–46.

point on his Lordship because every knee will bow and every tongue will confess to the glory of God the Father that Jesus is Lord (Phil 2:9–11).

The Bridge of the Arts

The creative arts can be an effective bridge to connect people with the gospel. Paul quoted the poets from Athens who would say, "For we are indeed his offspring" (Acts 17:28). This popular phrase became Paul's pivot point to share the gospel and humanity's need for repentance. God may use a line from a popular poet or a secular songwriter to open someone's heart. The poet's beautiful words, the guitar player's masterful chord arrangement, the storyteller's story, or the painter's contrast of colors all can serve as spiritual bridges while providing a glimpse of God's beauty. Francis Schaeffer wrote:

> For a Christian, redeemed by the work of Christ and living within the norms of Scripture and under the leadership of the Holy Spirit, the lordship of Christ should include an interest in the arts. A Christian should use these arts to the glory of God—not just as tracts, but as things of beauty to the praise of God.[11]

My friend Kerry Jackson is an example of an accomplished artist who has faithfully served as a missionary to other creatives. He uses his artistic abilities to build bridges for lost people to cross over to faith in Christ. He has a ministry called Drawing to the Rock and uses his studio in Marietta, Georgia, as a base for his mission. I've seen him have gospel conversations with people who would never have walked through the doors of a traditional church. God is using him and can use you in similar ways as well.

---

[11] Francis A. Schaeffer, *Art and the Bible* (Downers Grove, IL: Intervarsity Press, 1973), 18.

The Bridge of the Marketplace

Paul stepped outside the synagogue and walked among the philosophers in the marketplace. There is a parallel between the marketplace in Acts and the workplace of today. Billy Graham said, "I believe one of the next great moves of God is going to be through the believers in the workplace."[12] The book of Acts gives us multiple examples of the gospel penetrating the marketplace: stories of government officials, prisoners and jailers, military personnel, businesswomen, and tentmakers.

In New York City, Jeremiah Lanphier, in what some call the Third Great Awakening, forged connections through the workplace as well. Historian Randall Balmer writes:

> Lanphier, a man of considerable piety, organized what became known as the FULTON STREET PRAYER MEETING in an effort to reach the businessmen in lower Manhattan. On September 23, 1857, he began weekly prayer meetings at noon. As the REVIVAL caught on, the weekly meetings became daily, and they formed what was known as the PRAYER MEETING REVIVAL of 1857–1859.[13]

This awakening spread throughout the states into the far regions, and a nation observed what can happen when an everyday Christ follower chooses to engage the culture for the sake of the gospel.

The Bridge of God's Miracles

In Acts, a good number of the spiritual bridges that led to people accepting Jesus were signs and wonders. According to the Bible, God is able to heal people of their diseases and sicknesses. He still delivers people from

---

[12] Billy Graham, preface in Os Hillman, *His Presence in the Workplace Conference Manual* (Asheville, NC: Billy Graham Training Center, 2003), 1.

[13] Randall H. Balmer, *The Encyclopedia of Evangelicalism* (Philadelphia: Westminster, 2002), 330.

demonic possession and oppression. Jesus even said in John 14:11: "Believe me that I am in the Father and the Father is in me. Otherwise, believe because of the works themselves." Miracles can serve to prove the power and sovereignty of God. They invade our reality and turn our worlds upside right. They are obviously not an end unto themselves or meant to be the main event. Instead they graciously point us directly to the life-changing power and salvation of Jesus. The greatest miracle of all is when a person receives Christ, turning from idols to serve the living God. That's why we build spiritual bridges.

A miraculous move of God is happening across North America among college students. These modern Athens-type cities—college communities—are fertile fields to plant the gospel and new churches. God is using churches like Cornerstone in Ames, Iowa, to intentionally engage students with the gospel. Mark Vance, Salt Company director said, "Cornerstone made the commitment to be a church that puts college students on the front of the bus." They resolved to "never quit being the church that loves university students," and embedded in their ethos that they never fail to "win at reaching the campus."

This is an exemplary church that built a bridge to span the barriers that tend to hold back so many other churches from reaching students. By God's grace, the Salt Company ministries has grown to involve an average of 1,300 students on a weekly basis with 280 students serving as campus leaders. Cornerstone Church has grown to 2,500 people who attend their weekend services. God is using this church located in the heart of the nation to influence other campus ministries and collegiate church planting efforts all over the United States and Canada.[14] For example, they and other churches like them (H20 in Columbus, Ohio, and Resonate in Pullman, Washington)

---

[14] Mark Vance and Bryan Frye, "Church Planting in College Towns: From Ames, to Iowa City, to the End for the Earth," North American Mission Board, November 24, 2015, https://www.namb.net/news/church-planting-in-college-towns-from-ames-to-iowa-city-to-the-end-for-the-earth. For further information see the website of Cornerstone Church in Ames, Iowa: https://cornerstonelife.com/.

are sending teams of students upon their graduation to plant churches near other universities to see more people miraculously cross the bridge from unbelief to belief in Christ.

Conclusion

Although we don't read of great numbers who come to the Lord in the collegiate city of Athens, we do hear of Dionysius the Areopagite, a woman named Damaris, and others who believed (Acts 17:34). We also hear of those who ridiculed and rejected the message, and there were others who remained open to hearing more about the gospel. These three gospel responses were labeled by Adrian Rogers as decision, derision, and delay.[15] You and I can expect to encounter these three responses as well.

As you are on mission in your Athens, remember the results are in God's hands. Refuse to give up and burn bridges when a person does not respond immediately. God will continue to work according to his grace and mercy. Author Gary Comer writes about a simple approach to connecting with people the same way Jesus did. He states, "Soul whispering is the term I use to depict the mission manner of Christ. Jesus is the soul whisperer. Ever notice how He never gives the same presentation twice; but rather speaks personally and powerfully into each soul?"[16] The gospel is best shared not in a preplanned sales pitch or canned formula approach but through the discovery of the appropriate spiritual bridges. This is good counsel for all of us as we learn to build life-changing bridges.

---

[15] Adrian Rogers, "Standing Firm in a Pagan World: Acts 17:16–18" (sermon), Love Worth Finding, December 17, 2018, https://www.lwf.org/sermons/audio/standing-firm-in-a-pagan-world-2456.

[16] "Gary Comer—Soul Whisperer," *Kathy Harris: Writing to the Rhythm of a New Song* (blog), accessed May 31, 2019, https://kathyharrisbooks.com/gary-comer-the-soul-whisperer/. For more information see Gary Comer, *Soul Whisperer: Why the Church Must Change the Way It Views Evangelism* (Eugene, OR: Wipf and Stock, 2013).

Acts Immersion

Acts Action Item

Look for the points of connection in your culture individually and within your church.

Culture Change: Spiritual Bridges and Time

Sometimes it just takes time to see revival or the application of an idea manifest. Though God works on his timetable, given time, the consistent application of spiritual bridges can lead to a culture change in your church. It involves a new way of missional engagement or a paradigm shift. The story of the Seven Bridges in the city of Konigsberg, Prussia (now Kaliningrad, Russia), is a good illustration of time and paradigm shift.[17] The citizens had devised a puzzle. They asked, "Could a person cross all seven bridges by crossing each one exactly once?"

Leonhard Euler, the great mathematician, stepped back and observed the problem from a new paradigm by charting the points and creating a simple path. He viewed the puzzle as a graph. Although he resolved that it was unsolvable, he launched a new field of mathematics—called Graph Theory—as a result of his attempts to solve the puzzle. Centuries later this led to DNA sequencing through using—you guessed it—the simple Eulerian Path. It has allowed genetic scientists to decode enormous amounts of bioinformatics contained within DNA. Even now, a new field of algorithmic biology exists tracing its origins back to Seven Bridges in a Prussian

---

[17] RUDN University, "From Konigsberg Bridges to Genome Sequencing," a "science documentary telling a story of a single mathematical problem that makes its way to the fundamental theory of modern science," YouTube video, 10:08, published August 22, 2016, https://www.youtube.com/watch?v=cnYdRF99oJ8.

city.[18] Observe the bridges in your mission field, intentionally cross over them, and then give God time to work in the hearts of his people.

Acts Character and Competence

Be...

- stirred—by the idols in the city and the eternal destiny of those apart from Jesus Christ
- engaged—seeking out and creatively finding points of connection to the culture
- faithful—to the whole gospel message sharing the elements of repentance (life change) and resurrection

Know...

- that, like Paul, we ought to be stirred to action because of a city full of idols
- that spiritual bridges are points of contact for the gospel
- that sinful culture should be engaged but not embraced by the missionary—Christians are to be in the world but not of it (John 17:11)
- that spiritual bridges move a person from the known to the unknown—point lost people to repentance and belief in the resurrected Christ

Do...

- Prayerfully read the daily devotional "Acts Moment" and the Acts Bible readings below.
- Look for points of connection that might serve as spiritual bridges.

---

[18] Natalia Deryugina, "From Konigsberg Bridges to Genome Sequencing," Algorithimic Biology Lab, St. Petersburg Academic University, interview with Yana Pachkovskaya.

- Ask God to fill you with his Holy Spirit afresh and anew to be his witness.
- Recommit to living a godly life of character and uncompromising belief.
- Commit to be at the corporate prayer time this week.
- Commit to utilize the *ACTS Prayer Guide* at the weekly corporate prayer or your personal prayer time.

Acts Reading

Day 1: Acts 15:1–35
Day 2: Acts 15:36–41
Day 3: Acts 16:1–5
Day 4: Acts 16:6–10
Day 5: Acts 16:11–40

Acts Missionary Activity

Spiritual Bridges: A Stirred Heart and Crossing Cultural Bridges

Plan to go to a mall or a department store this week. Walk around with an eye to observe the idols of our culture. Focus on one that stirs your heart and think about how you might engage a person who worships this idol. Consider what their spiritual bridge may be. If God gives the opportunity, find someone to engage using your bridge.

Reflection: What did God do in your heart as you observed the idols?

Spiritual Bridges in the Life of Christ

Jesus modeled spiritual bridges foremost in his incarnation. He was a friend of sinners yet without sin. His parables were stories that went from the known to the unknown in the spiritual realm. His miracles served as spiritual bridges to teach eternal lessons and call people to follow him.

For Further Reading

- *Bridges of God* by Donald McGavran
- *How to Know God Exists* by Ray Comfort
- *The Reason for God* by Tim Keller

9

Spiritual Giftedness: Gather and Give Resources from the Harvest
(Corinth)

> *A person should think of us in this way: as servants of Christ and managers of the mysteries of God. In this regard, it is required that managers be found faithful.*
> —1 Corinthians 4:1–2

> *In fact, one of the laws of the harvest (to which the church's task is likened) says, "The resources are in the harvest." (In the harvest," where the church planter is sent to labor, the resources will be found for the congregation's future.)*
> —Charles Chaney, *Church Planting at the End of the Twentieth Century*

It was a stroke of marketing genius to portray DNA tests as the ideal gift to give to yourself or someone you love. In 2017, 1.5 million testing kits were sold between Black Friday and Cyber Monday.[1] Obviously many people are curious about their genetic makeup, including how it can serve them, and, interestingly, this holds several parallels to how Christians view spiritual giftedness. For example, many folks think of genetic testing as a fun party game, something that's interesting but not all that practical. This is, unfortunately, very much like how some believers incorrectly view the concept of spiritual giftedness. They're delighted to know they have the gift of such-and-such, but the missional aspect and stewardship of their gifting is completely lost on them.

Another parallel between the wonder of DNA testing and how Christians view spiritual giftedness is the explosion—a modern-day gold rush of sorts—that the new field of genetics has opened. For some, genetic testing is only about selfishly padding their wallets while for others it's truly about giving back to the world through advances in science. Likewise, some Christians view gifting and stewardship with curiosity and a subtle dose of selfishness while others are truly passionate about and generous toward supporting the mission of God. We dearly need to return to a biblical and missional understanding of spiritual giftedness because it is God who gives the resources that fuel the harvest.

The next strand of DNA, *spiritual giftedness*, is expressed in giving and gathering resources for and from the harvest. Spiritual giftedness includes the supernatural gifts of the Holy Spirit as well as our time, treasures, and talent. It is a reciprocal cycle of giving and gathering that occurs as we labor in our fields, evangelizing and discipling new believers. In Acts, the church at Corinth best exemplifies this principle, especially when you consider Paul's two letters to the Corinthian church.

---

[1] CBS News Online, "In Modern-Day Gold Rush of Genetic Testing, Profit Placed above Proof," *CBS This Morning*, February 10, 2016, https://www.cbsnews.com/news/cbs-news-investigation-genetic-tests-pathway-genomics-profit-over-evidence/.

The principle of spiritual giftedness begins with a commitment to share all that God has graciously given to us and our church. The beautiful thing is that these all flow supernaturally from out of the harvest. In the Lord's work, just like the genetic gold in the hills and in those profitable new DNA applications, the fields are already white for harvest with unclaimed supernatural and natural resources to be mined by his people on mission.

In 1995, God called us to Holiday Shores Baptist Church in Illinois. The church plant was blessed with a core group of people with a heart for the harvest. Intuitively, this group seemed to know that every future small group leader, every future deacon, every children's worker—absolutely everything God knew we needed—was already out there in the fields waiting to be claimed for Christ. New believers were won to Christ and then intentionally mobilized back into the harvest to evangelize and make more disciples. We didn't need all of the resources on day one. The resources we were about to need became available as people came to Christ.

The names of people God brought to his work in Illinois with just the right *talents*, skills, and experience flood my mind. Norman would always meet you at the door with a warm welcome and a smile. The countless hours of *time* people gave in service to the Lord were incredible. During my tenure, the church took on a building project. There were men like Ray, Mark, and Tim, along with a host of others, who led the way to see it to completion. Fred and Lori opened their home to host and lead a Bible study for couples. People discovered and used their *spiritual gifts*, like Gene, who administered our Sunday school. *Treasures* were given to the Lord, tangible and intangible, that were needed for ministry and mission. These are just a few of the many names and examples of people and things that came directly from God—the spiritual DNA of giftedness in action. The truth is God provides the fuel for the harvest *from* his harvest.

It's helpful in describing this principle to first look at its genetic mutation. This DNA strand in mutated form is a self-absorbed church that possesses a tightfisted attitude toward resources. For them, the solution to a problem such as a lack of volunteers or finances is not missional engagement.

Instead, missional engagement is only a religious duty to perform. In addition, decision-making is consistently based on consumer-oriented priorities. Evangelizing the lost and making disciples is rarely the priority. There can also be an unhealthy focus on the gifts without giving the proper attention to the Gift Giver or, in some cases, an outright neglect of spiritual gifts altogether. If taught at all, stewardship is only about money. Cheerful generosity is replaced with giving in a begrudging manner or not even giving at all.

The mutated church bemoans that their harvest fields are without workers and consequently that they are without the flow of resources that naturally comes from them. Their mentality is that the "lost can come find us." Spiritual gifts remain hidden and unexercised. Time is a wasted commodity. Rather than investing them into God's kingdom work, talents are spent on worldly things. Does this sound familiar? It is, sadly, very common in our churches today. But it wasn't meant to be this way. Let's look at what our church culture is meant to be, and how we can grow in our understanding and application of spiritual giftedness.

The Purpose of Spiritual Giftedness

To understand the purpose of spiritual giftedness, it's essential to begin with a foundational discussion regarding spiritual gifts. Spiritual gifts exist in service to the church—not for our agendas and not for our comfort. They are for building up the church and bringing the gospel message to the lost. Acts documents a special move of God as people willingly and generously expressed their spiritual giftedness for the Great Commission of Jesus. This move of God occured within the context of the church as the church went into the harvest fields.

Spiritual gifts are also found in the harvest. It was in the harvest fields where Jesus lovingly identified people's untapped potential. Consider who he chose: the fishermen, tax collectors, and prostitutes. These were individuals the world often deemed as small and insignificant, but they were transformed by Jesus and soon discovered their place in God's kingdom work. As we think about spiritual giftedness, don't overlook "the least of these."

Too, think of the little boy who gave his fish and bread to the disciples and then got to witness Jesus miraculously feed the multitudes. We need to remember there are resources *in* the harvest. We often think of taking up special collections from our local church, but there are plentiful resources *in* those we go to minister to. The offering plates extend well beyond the four walls of our churches.

In addition, spiritual giftedness is meant to have a multiplying effect. God's reality is different from what we see with our eyes. God multiplies small gifts to make a big impact. The poor widow gave her seemingly small offering—just two coins—and Jesus declared that she gave more than anyone else. In the parable of the talents, we see that God expects resources will be multiplied for the Master's pleasure (even if a person has only one talent). These are acts of generosity and stewardship, with resources holding up the standard of kingdom investment.

Spiritual gifts are practical in nature. Jesus explained how the basic resources for the missionary were already in the harvest—food, shelter, even cups of cold water (Matt 10:40–42). Jesus said, "Remain in the same house, eating and drinking what they offer, for the worker is worthy of his wages. Don't move from house to house" (Luke 10:7). He promised to take care of his servants while they served, and he will take care of you and me too.

Finally, spiritual gifts are to be shared generously. Matthew recorded, "Freely you received, freely give" (Matt 10:8b). God expects generous attitudes and actions to prevail among his missionary force. This was true for the first-century church and is true for us today. Take note, spiritual gifts are not about your strengths but about Christ's strength working in and through us. Barnabas is a powerful example of sharing gifts with selfless generosity. He set the bar high through his giving of resources and encouraging heart. He invested in relationships and helped others discover their gifts for the sake of the gospel. Barnabas followed the Jesus who he loved and served. His giving was simply a reflection of that.

The Gifts of the Spirit

With a foundation of how spiritual gifts operate, we turn now to what specifically is included when we talk about spiritual giftedness. First, spiritual giftedness obviously includes the actual spiritual gift or gifts given to new believers when the Holy Spirit indwells them. Paul wrote in Ephesians:

> Now grace was given to each one of us according to the measure of Christ's gift. For it says: When he ascended on high, he took the captives captive; he gave gifts to people. But what does "he ascended" mean except that he also descended to the lower parts of the earth? The one who descended is also the one who ascended far above all the heavens, to fill all things. And he himself gave some to be apostles, some prophets, some evangelists, some pastors and teachers, equipping the saints for the work of ministry, to build up the body of Christ, until we all reach unity in the faith and in the knowledge of God's Son, growing into maturity with a stature measured by Christ's fullness. (4:7–13)

Jesus ascended so that the Spirit—with his indwelling work and empowering gifts—could descend upon his people. When a person is born again, they receive the Holy Spirit and at least one of the spiritual gifts (1 Cor 12:1–31). Similar to your physical DNA, God's spiritual gift mix for you is unique.

The gifts of the Holy Spirit are spiritual resources that are truly game changers for us and our churches. If we submit to God and exercise our spiritual gifts, we will find ourselves in a position to be used by God on his mission. These spiritual gifts were given in list form in the New Testament and referred to within a number of passages:

Rom 12:6–8
Prophecy
Serving
Teaching
Exhortation
Giving
Leadership
Mercy

1 Cor 12:8–10
Word of wisdom
Word of knowledge
Faith
Gifts of healings
Miracles
Prophecy
Distinguishing between spirits
Tongues
Interpretation of tongues

1 Cor 12:28
Apostle
Prophet
Teacher
Miracles
Gifts of healings
Helps
Administration
Tongues

1 Pet 4:9–11
Hospitality
Speaking
Service

(These are not meant to be an exhaustive listing)

Lastly, in Eph 4:1–16, the fivefold offices of the church likewise imply spiritual giftedness. These offices were given with the function of equipping the saints for the work of the ministry. Although we do not have apostles in the sense of people who have literally been with Jesus, there is an apostolic gifting that is a vital function of the church—the missionary or sent one. Likewise, the office of the prophet is not necessarily exercised in the form of predicting the future as much as it is about speaking forth the truth in love. The application of these five gifts was intended to be a part of what leadership looks like in the local body of Christ. Leadership is to be shared and balanced with gifts. Each one who has one of these callings is intended to equip and mobilze others to live like missionaries, prophets, evangelists, shepherds, and teachers in their spheres of influence. Here is a listing of these callings:

- Apostle—pioneering missions
- Prophet—forthtelling
- Evangelist—sharing Christ
- Shepherd—pastoral care
- Teacher—communicating truth

In the Corinth church plant story, we see several of the spiritual gifts: service, preaching, teaching, evangelism, discernment, apostolic mission, leadership, and shepherding (Acts 18:1–17). Each church plant in Acts pointed to members with a healthy array of spiritual gifts and a compelling witness to how God called ordinary people to be on mission.

The Holy Spirit is God and he will not be manipulated for selfish ends. He can choose to use you and your spiritual gifts. Over the years, there has been much abuse within the church related to spiritual gifts. This happened in the church at Corinth too. In fact, Paul's first epistle was written to them in order to deal with their disunity, immorality, false doctrine, and abuse of the gifts. When abuse happens, we can find ourselves turning away from and suspicious of the gifts. Consequently, people tend to rush to the extremes of what has been called by some as charisphobia or charismania. But the truth is all spiritual gifts are for building up the church.

While spiritual gifts are the foundation for this DNA principle, there are three additional general groupings of giftedness that Luke alludes to in Acts 18:1–10: time, talent, and treasure. All three of these are seen within the harvest fields of Corinth.

The Gift of Time

Time is likely our most precious commodity and often our most misused. In the story at Corinth, God sovereignly prepared the husband-and-wife team Aquila and Priscilla to be in town ahead of Paul's arrival. Claudius had ordered all of the Jews to leave Rome (Acts 18:2), but it was and is ultimately God who orchestrates the strategic timing and placement of people.

God then provides the team with a marketplace platform of tentmaking—once again ordaining time for spiritual sowing, spiritual bridge building, and a means of supporting their ministry.

We also see in the story of Corinth that there is a time limit to our efforts sharing the gospel with people. Luke recorded, "When they resisted and blasphemed, he [Paul] shook out his clothes and told them, 'Your blood is on your own heads! I am innocent. From now on I will go to the Gentiles'" (Acts 18:6). The phrase "from now on" is a statement of obedience on his part and urgency to Jesus's instruction to not delay or spin our wheels with people who reject the message. Jesus was clear that time is precious and we are to keep looking for those who will hear and receive the gospel (Matt 10:14; Mark 6:11).

God also uses the gift of time to speak profound words of direction and encouragement to us at precisely the right moment. After a difficult season sharing the gospel in Corinth, "The Lord said to Paul in a night vision, 'Don't be afraid, but keep on speaking and don't be silent. For I am with you, and no one will lay a hand on you to hurt you, because I have many people in this city" (Acts 18:9–10). In a dark time, this word from God served to remind Paul that God was with him and that Paul's work was important. Sometimes God gives us encouraging words directly and sometimes they come through the Word or through other people. As we give our time to God, God provides us with exactly what we need when we need it.

Though time is a gift, we often dismiss its fleetingness or use it for our own pleasure. Paul decided to stay in Corinth for a year and a half to teach the people who were new in the faith (Acts 18:11). This was a long time for him compared to other cities in their journeys. It is not true that everyone has the same amount of time on their clocks, days on their calendars, or years in their lives. Tomorrow is not promised to anyone. Though we forget or become distracted, God expects us to invest our time in evangelizing, making disciples, and being on mission. What we do with our time on earth makes the difference for eternity.

The Gift of Treasures

We also have the gift of treasure. Though monetary wealth is certainly included, our treasure includes more than our finances. The first and foremost treasure in the harvest is the assurance that Jesus is always with us. Not for a moment are we without him. God told Paul that he could be fearless to keep speaking for Christ because Jesus promised his presence and protection (Matt 28:20). Also, God reminded Paul that he was already at work and had many other people in Corinth (Acts 18:10–11). The mission is always bigger than what one person can see and you can be confident that God is at work in ways not seen or totally understood. Alongside the treasure of his presence is the treasure of the Word of God, the special revelation bringing encouragement, instruction, and challenge to us. The Word of God is alive and our missional lifeline. The Spirit brings life to us through the Word. No word from God is ever wasted in God's economy and no promise of God goes unfulfilled.

People are another treasure. Aquila and Priscilla would go on to travel with Paul to Ephesus, speak into Apollos's life, and later start a church in their home (Acts 18:24–28; Rom 16:3–5a). Titius Justus lived next door to the synagogue. He was described as a worshiper of God and more than likely a person of peace. He opened his home to become another place of ministry (Acts 18:7). Crispus, the leader of the synagogue, and his household came to faith in Jesus and his home was mentioned as another base of operation—even the ordinance of baptism was performed there. We all have Aquilas, Priscillas, Titiuses, and Crispuses in our lives, people prepared by God to open their hearts to his mission and in turn open their relational networks for the gospel. People who serve the body and bring encouragement. And people from whom new leadership comes.

As you trace the DNA strand of spiritual giftedness through Acts, we discover the list is centered on people who have something to give: homes, gifts, and finances. Barnabas sold property and gave its proceeds to the church. The first deacons ensured care for the Grecian widows. Cornelius, Lydia, Titius Justus, and Crispus opened up their homes. The church at

Antioch gave generously during a severe famine. One of the main themes of the second epistle to the Corinthians is that of generosity and stewardship. They were a church blessed with a treasure of financial resources. However, the primary resource was and always will be the people of God—they gave of themselves first to the Lord.

Each time you pick up a penny, remember to "trust in God" as inscribed on the coin. It is also a reminder of the way God sees and values all people. Picking up a penny is a regular practice for me and serves as a spiritual trigger for me to think about what Jesus said about a lost coin and the rejoicing that happens when it is found. Author G. K. Chesterton said:

> People are equal in the same way pennies are equal. Some are bright, others are dull; some are worn smooth, others are sharp and fresh. But all are equal in value for each penny bears the image of the sovereign, each person bears the image of the King of Kings.[2]

The people in our lives are incredible treasures. Every blood-bought Christian has the Holy Spirit living inside of them and has something of incredible value to give to the Lord, starting with their lives in devotion to Christ. Every person without Christ is someone he shed his blood for and we have a serious responsibility and blessed privilege to share the gospel with them.

The DNA principle of spiritual giftedness is expressed by abounding in every good work with the resources God graciously gives (2 Cor 9:8). We have the Holy Spirit. We have the Word. We have the people in our mission fields. We also usually have more than we need in our homes and bank accounts. David Platt writes, "The Bible teaches that God gives us more not so that we can have more, but so we can give more."[3] The church on mission will be a generous church, consistently demonstrating mercy to those

---

[2] Quoted in Duncan B. Forrester, *On Human Worth: A Christian Vindication of Equality* (London: SCM Press, 2001), 46.

[3] David Platt, *Counter Culture: Following Christ in an Anti-Christian Age* (Carol Stream, IL: Tyndale House, 2011), 41.

in need through giving their treasures (Acts 4:32–37; 6:1–7; 11:27–30; 20:33–35).

The Gift of Talents

Paul met and joined with Aquila and Priscilla, who, like him, were tent-makers by trade. God can powerfully use the one who is willing to take a secular occupation to build spiritual bridges in a community and be occupied with the gospel testimony (Acts 18:5). These people are modern day heroes of the faith who support their ministry by a specific occupation. Those pastors, church leaders, and church members who do it well have learned how to balance life and mission. There is a great blessing in using vocation for mission because gospel engagement is natural in the workplace. Whether Paul was bi-vocational by necessity or by strategic choice, it was without question a holy calling for him. Paul described this holy calling and all it involved with much detail in the second epistle to the church at Corinth (1 Cor 9:1–27). We all have talents and we all have platforms. Let's use what we have for the gospel.

Hospitality is also a way we can offer ourselves to our neighbors. So much of ministry in Acts started in the marketplace and quickly moved to the homes of new Christ followers. Hospitality is definitely listed as a spiritual gift and at the same time it's a command to be followed by all believers. The person who exercises this gift equips believers to serve others well with Christian hospitality, thus multiplying themselves (see 1 Pet 4:9 and Rom 12:13). We must be willing to host others and enter the homes of others for gospel engagement. Look at Jesus's example. Author Tim Chester observed, "In Luke's Gospel, Jesus is either going to a meal, at a meal, or coming from a meal."[4] The notion of loving your neighbor as you love yourself is not a lofty, unattainable platitude. Jesus redefined "your neighbor." He described

---

[4] Tim Chester, *A Meal with Jesus: Discovering Grace, Community, and Mission around the Table* (Wheaton, IL: Crossway, 2011), 13.

a neighbor as someone who shows mercy to anyone in need. The story of the Good Samaritan shows us a man offering his time, talent, and treasure. He was interruptable. He gave freely of what he had to help someone in need. Hospitality in the home is much the same.

In Corinth, each person used their God-given abilities. God expects a proportionate return on his investment of talents. In the parable of the talents (Matt 25:14–30), Jesus was pleased with the man who had two talents and multiplied them to four. He was pleased with the man who had five talents and multiplied them to ten. Do you see the pattern? The man who had only one talent buried it. Because he failed to use his talent in service to the kingdom, he lost everything and was thrown into the outer darkness. The master described him as wicked and slothful.

The parable is about faithful obedience to the Master. Salvation is based on Christ's grace. It is not based on how one handles or mishandles their talent(s), but it would be illustrative to say that there are five, two, and one talent Christians and churches. The problem is not in comparable abilities but in wicked disbelief and lazy attitudes regarding mission. If we are not evangelizing and making disciples, we need to think carefully about the implication of this parable. True believers produce or bear fruit. When we use our talents for God's mission, we will experience indescribable joy and great reward (Matt 25:21).

Spiritual Giftedness in the Church Today

Ferris Hill Baptist located in Milton, Florida, does spiritual giftedness well. The small church—though not small in God's eyes—is in the middle of a community with widespread poverty issues. They are not a church with an abundance of finances, and yet they describe themselves as a church with a *sufficiency* of finances to sustain the various ministries. The church has a "Love Thy Neighbor" food distribution ministry. They have their county's only cold weather shelter for the homeless. The church also regularly serves the poor in Haiti. On one occasion, a building in Haiti needed a new roof.

The church sprung into action, calling for a special offering. Former Pastor Brian Nall joyfully said, "We met our goal in about ten minutes, quickly doubled it, and then I had to say, 'stop giving!'" In addition, the church serves through an I-58 Ministry, which is based on reaching out to the poor as the prophet Isaiah exhortated in chapter 58. Their focus is on the things God described as real religion: the compassionate actions of feeding, clothing, sheltering, or providing transportation for people in need.

Pastor Nall stated, "Over the past decade Ferris Hill has seen the generosity of God reflected in our people and spill over into generosity in our community. Every step of the way we have been reminded that we cannot out-give God." Their giving and mission involvement has doubled because they see themselves as a "conduit of generosity." Pastor Brian reminds us, "When you give generously according to the principles of God's Holy Word, you end up planting seeds into other people's lives and the opportunities lead to a harvest of blessings in the future. Seed planting first, harvest later."[5] This is the whole point of spiritual giftedness.

Conclusion

Optics (or how people perceive us) is a popular word and idea in our time. Many of us choose to be passionate about our public perception—the size of our social media following, the busyness of our schedule and church events calendar, the type of car we drive—as well as how to stay comfortable in our current circumstances. But imagine a church who specializes in radical obedience and generosity. It

- Becomes a force for meeting human needs with the resources from the harvest.

---

[5] Brian Nall, *An Uphill Journey: One Small Church's Journey to Revitalization* (Orlando, FL Renovate, 2016); personal interview and email correspondence May 21, 2015.

- Uses the resources from the harvest to reach the nations with the gospel.
- Exercises the spiritual gifts gleaned from the harvest to build up the body of Christ.
- Invests the resources of time, talent, and treasure from the harvest to reach the lost in their community.

This is the church in the book of Acts.

The heartbreaking fact is that most churches have genetically mutated in this area. A story from the seventeenth century illustrates this point. St. Francis of Assisi held an interview with Pope Honorius II about the Catholic Church and its resources. Honorius showed St. Francis the rooms filled with treasure that the church had accumulated over the centuries, saying, "We can no longer say 'Silver and gold have I none.'" St. Francis then responded, "And neither can we say 'Take up your bed and walk.'"[6] Both men referenced the same scripture (Acts 3:6, from the healing of the lame man at the temple gate), but they had very different views of spiritual giftedness. Dan Olson from the Gospel Coalition writes:

> When I describe radical generosity, I'm talking about joyfully giving all of one's time, talent, and treasures for the sake of God's kingdom and a heavenly reward, without expecting any (earthly) return on investment.[7]

In other words, a church on mission consciously relinquishes the need to hoard resources, but instead freely distributes God-given resources according to the leading and power of the Holy Spirit. The church on mission today must operate in the same biblical pattern of generosity as they did in Acts. When we do this, we will see God move in extraordinary ways.

---

[6] There are multiple versions of this story that either involve St. Francis or St. Aquinas.

[7] Dan Olson, "The Time Is Ripe for Radical Generosity," *Gospel Coalition Blog*, December 26, 2014, http://relevantchristian.com/the-gospel-coalition-blog/4753-the-time-is-ripe-for-radical-generosity.html.

Acts Immersion

Acts Action Item

Commit to sharing the resources God has given you in your life and the life of your church.

Culture Change: Spiritual Giftedness and Experiences

Intentional missionary experiences have the potential to change you and your church's missional culture. Scientists have discovered that experiences in your life can change gene expression and leave a lasting marker on your physical DNA. Experiences can flip the switch inside our genes and potentially heal all kinds of diseases and genetic disorders.[8]

On the other hand, researchers have discovered that traumatic experiences can affect physical DNA, even negatively touching future generations. As a result, educators are understanding the importance of trauma-informed learning for students. A traumatized child has a chemical change occurring on the molecular DNA level in their body and this adversely affects the student's ability to learn.[9] Experiences (good or bad) can literally change a person at even the molecular level!

My desire is for you to have positive missionary experiences through this time of missional revival. Each week, you are asked to engage in an activity designed to assist you in applying the spiritual DNA principles. My prayer is these experiences will "flip the switch" in your heart and draw you closer to God's kingdom purpose. Think about Paul in the city of Corinth

---

[8] James Eberwine, "Experience Changes Gene Expression," DNA Learning Center, accessed May 9, 2016, https://www.dnalc.org/view/2068-Experience-changes-gene-expression.html.

[9] Nadine Burke Harris, "How Childhood Trauma Affects Health across a Lifetime," TED talk, September 2014, https://www.ted.com/talks/nadine_burke_harris_how_childhood_trauma_affects_health_across_a_lifetime.

and how he experienced the elements of spiritual giftedness as he engaged the people there. As you move out of your comfort zone, God will use the challenges to create a holy space to do a deep work in your walk with him (if it's possible, even to the molecular level), and reveal his glory through your life on mission like he did for Paul.

Acts Character and Competence

Be...

- available—use your vocation to share the gospel and start churches
- generous—share the resources God has given you
- sent—go into the harvest field expecting God to provide

Know...

- that spiritual resources are already in the harvest—spiritual gifts, time, talents, and treasures
- that people are among the greatest resources in missions and church planting
- that Corinth was a spiritually gifted church with strong leaders, diverse gifts, and financial means

Do...

- Prayerfully read the daily devotional "Acts Moment" and the Acts Bible readings.
- Open your home to start a small group or host a meal to reach out to the lost.
- Take a spiritual gifts inventory or ask someone to help you discover your spiritual gift mix.
- Determine to utilize your time, treasure, or talents for God's glory and his missions.
- Commit to be at the corporate prayer time this week.
- Ask God to fill you with His Holy Spirit afresh and anew to be his witness.

- Commit to utilize the *ACTS Prayer Guide* at the weekly corporate prayer or your personal prayer time.

Acts Reading

Day 1: Acts 17:1–9
Day 2: Acts 17:10–15
Day 3: Acts 17:16–34
Day 4: Acts 18:1–17
Day 5: Acts 18:18–28

Acts Missionary Activity

Spiritual Giftedness: Open Your Home—Hospitality

Invite an unreached neighbor into your home for a meal or for coffee and dessert this week. Talk to them about their interests and giftedness. Be a good listener and host. Be sure to pray with them.

Reflection: What did you learn about your neighbor and what he or she could potentially give to God's kingdom mission? Time, talents, treasure . . . if a believer what about spiritual gifts?

Spiritual Giftedness in the Life of Christ

Jesus freely gave of his time, talents, and treasure for those in need. He spoke often about caring for the poor and found ways to minister to them. He taught stewardship and generosity through his parables.

For Further Reading

- *The Treasure Principle* by Randy Alcorn
- *Spiritual Gifts* by Thomas Schreiner
- *What's So Spiritual About Your Gifts* by Henry Blackaby and Mel Blackaby

10

Spiritual Warfare: Fight the Good Fight
(Ephesus)

For our struggle is not against flesh and blood, but against the rulers, against the authorities, against the cosmic powers of this darkness, against evil, spiritual forces in the heavens.
—Ephesians 6:12

Spiritual warfare, the conflict of two opposing wills—namely that of God and his followers versus Satan and his followers.
—John Franklin and Chuck Lawless, *Spiritual Warfare: Biblical Truth for Victory*

In 1986, the first-ever DNA evidence brought about the conviction of a criminal. Alec Jeffreys, a professor from the University of Leicester, England was the first to pioneer the idea of DNA profiling.[1] During an earlier failed

---

[1] Stuart H. James and Jon J. Nordby, *Forensic Science: An Introduction to Scientific and Investigative Techniques* (Boca Raton, FL: CRC Press, 2005), 284. For further reading, see Ian Cobain, "Killer Breakthrough—the Day DNA Evidence First Nailed a Murder," *Guardian* (UK), June 7, 2016, https://www

experiment attempting to trace heredity, Jeffreys discovered that DNA has a unique fingerprint. In the criminal case, police had mistakenly charged Richard Buckland, a seventeen-year-old boy with learning disabilities, of murder. He was later cleared by Jeffreys's DNA fingerprinting. This inspired police to test all of the men in the village which, in turn, led to the arrest and conviction of the real killer. Today DNA is used every day in investigations and courtroom proceedings to fight the good fight against injustice.

This battle for truth is not unlike the battle Christians face in spiritual warfare. *Spiritual warfare* is the last strand of the DNA of a church on mission. The church at Ephesus gives us a first-hand glimpse of what this principle can look like (Acts 18:20–28; 19:1–4; 20:17–38). The missionary team there faced demonic ploys and sinister attacks—and as always, the spiritual stakes were very high. Francis Schaeffer said, "We are locked in a battle. This is not a friendly gentleman's discussion. It is a life and death conflict between the spiritual hosts of wickedness and those who claim the name of Christ."[2] Spiritual warfare is serious business.

There are only two sources of everything encountered in this life—the kingdom of light and the kingdom of darkness. If you answer the call to evangelize, make disciples, and plant churches you will be positioned on the frontlines of the battle between these two kingdoms. The decision to be on mission with God is always a war cry against the devil and a bold counter-offensive move.

There are many Christians who do not know their identity in Christ or the devil's tactics to thwart the advance of God's kingdom. Elmer Towns aptly comments, "The Apostle Paul once wrote, 'Lest Satan should get an advantage of us: for we are not ignorant of his devices'" (2 Cor 2:11). It must be sadly concluded, however, that many of us are, and therefore he

---

.theguardian.com/uk-news/2016/jun/07/killer-dna-evidence-genetic-profiling-criminal-investigation.

[2] Francis A. Schaeffer, *The Evangelical Disaster* (Wheaton, IL: Crossway, 1984), 31.

has."[3] Ignorance too often reigns in the twenty-first-century church. Let this not be the case for us as we explore spiritual warfare.

The Purpose of Spiritual Warfare

In his book *The Devil Goes to Church*, David Butts writes, "Though spiritual warfare is a reality that cannot be avoided, the real value of studying this issue is that it drives us to Jesus."[4] Nothing can send us more quickly into a deeper relationship with Christ than spiritual warfare. Scripture makes clear we will win. First John 4:4 says, "You are from God, little children, and you have conquered them, because the one who is in you is greater than the one who is in the world." Even with the outcome known, however, each battle requires our time, energy, and precise focus.

Jesus battled Satan from the temptation in the wilderness all the way to the week of his passion and the laying down of his life on the cross. Jesus was tempted in every way as we are but never once committed a sin. His life provides us with living lessons on how to overcome in the spiritual battles encountered every day.

- Jesus was tempted by Satan to use his divine power for selfish ends. "If you are the Son of God, tell these stones to become bread," Satan taunted (Matt 4:3). And again on the cross: "If you are the Son of God, come down from the cross!" (27:40). Jesus resisted.
- Jesus was tempted by Satan to go a different way from the cross. "I [the devil] will give you all these things if you will fall down and worship me" (Matt 4:9). And again in the Garden of Gethsemane Jesus prayed that the cup of the cross would pass from him. Yet he boldly determined not to do his will but the will of his Father.

---

[3] Elmer Towns, "Satan (the Devil)—the Enemy of God," BibleSprout (2015), accessed June 22, 2016, https://www.biblesprout.com/articles/hell/satan-devil/.

[4] David Butts, *The Devil Goes to Church: Prayer as Spiritual Warfare* (Terre Haute, IN: Prayer Shop, 2000), 89.

- Jesus was tempted by Satan to presume upon God by jumping off the pinnacle of the temple. "Let the angels catch you!" the devil said. At Jesus's arrest, he said to those surrounding him that he could have called down 10,000 angels to deliver him but instead he followed the Father's plan to the cross.

Jesus knows exactly what it's like to be tempted by the flesh (appetites), pride of life (ambition), and the world (allegiances). He also knows what it's like to overcome temptation by staying focused on the mission, relying on the power of the Word of God, and walking in an intimate relationship with his heavenly Father.

My Grandma Hazel taught me about spiritual warfare and the importance of fighting the good fight of faith. On more than one occasion, I'd share with her about the struggles of ministry. She would confidently respond by saying, "Have faith in God, because he can move those mountains in your life" (see Mark 11:22). This was one of her favorite verses. Little did I know at the time that she was teaching me about the main weapons of our warfare: prayer and the Word of God. After I became an adult, I learned how difficult her life had been. She had grown up during the Great Depression. When she was young, her father was struck by lightning and died. Later in life her husband left her to raise four young children on her own. Yet through all the seemingly debilitating spiritual battles, God continually moved the mountains in her life. She reminded me that if I am doing what God wants me to do, then I will inevitably make the devil mad.

Christ followers ought to expect opposition. She taught me that we never know how big of a threat we are to the enemy until we start to do something for God. It's much like the *Far Side* cartoon of a deer with a bull's-eye on its side. A fellow deer looks at the bull's-eye and remarks, "Bummer of a birthmark, Hal!"[5] It's no different for the individual and church on mission: you and I have a target on our backs. Author Charles Mylander writes, "Ignorance is not bliss, it is defeat. If you are a Christian,

---

[5] Gary Larson, *Far Side Gallery 2* (n.p.: Gary Larson, 1986).

you are a target. If you are a pastor, you and your family are in the bull's-eye."[6] Take heart though because believers have access to the full armor of God and all the weapons of spiritual warfare. Paul explains how in his letter to the Ephesians.

Writing to the church at Ephesus, Paul instructs them to not give the devil a foothold or opportunity (Eph 4:27). He later warned them against participating "in the fruitless works of darkness" but instead to "expose them" (Eph 5:11). And then he told them how to prepare for battle:

> Finally, be strengthened by the Lord and by his vast strength. Put on the full armor of God so that you can stand against the schemes of the devil. For our struggle is not against flesh and blood but against the rulers, against the authorities, against the cosmic powers of this darkness, against evil, spiritual forces in the heavens. For this reason take up the full armor of God, so that you may be able to resist in the evil day, and having prepared everything, to take your stand. (Eph 6:10–13)

Paul then goes on to list the armor: truth, righteousness, the gospel of peace, faith, salvation, the word of God, prayer, staying alert, perseverance, interceding for the saints, and praying for boldness (Eph 6:14–20). The truth is, by the grace of God, we have everything we need for the battle. Chuck Lawless boldly states:

> Spiritual warfare is not about reacting to the enemy—it is about putting on the armor of God in preparation for the battle. The church, rather than the enemy, possesses the upper hand in the battle by standing armed against the devil's attacks.[7]

---

[6] Neil T. Anderson and Charles Mylander, *Setting Your Church Free: A Biblical Plan to Help Your Church* (Ventura, CA: Regal Books, 1999), 24.

[7] Chuck E. Lawless, *Disciple Warriors: Growing Healthy Churches That Are Equipped for Spiritual Warfare* (Grand Rapids: Kregel, 2002), 18.

This battle-ready attitude leads us to becoming fearless and intrepid men and women on mission. Out of all the stories in Acts, the people from Ephesus appeared to be the most influenced by this satanic oppression, but everything dramatically changes when the gospel comes. The good news of Jesus teaches us the battle is won. Let us be keenly aware, however, of the strategies of the enemy so that we stand firm.

Spiritual Warfare against Misinformation

All through Acts we see Paul, Barnabas, and the team doing extensive teaching. Clearly, sound doctrine and understanding is important to God. One of Satan's primary tactics is to launch misinformation campaigns against God's people. Spiritual warfare is oftentimes at its most intense when dealing with doctrinal error or incomplete teaching. When a person's salvation or focus is at stake, the devil and his scheming forces will use all manner of propaganda to thwart God's mission. A telltale sign of a misinformation campaign is that it leads people away from the mission of God and the role of the Holy Spirit in mission (Matt 18:19–20; Acts 1:8).

For example, in Lystra people spread word that Paul and Barnabas were actually the gods Hermes and Zeus visiting them (Acts 13:8–20). In Ephesus, the young orator Apollos misunderstood the Messiahship of Jesus, and John the Baptist's disciples misunderstooad aspects of the Holy Spirit (Acts 18:24–28; 19:1–7). Military leaders know the importance of clear communication. Likewise, in spiritual warfare clear communication puts God's people in the best possible position to succeed and avoid the painful fallout from an inaccurate understanding of truth.

Another telltale sign of misinformation is that the teaching questions the authority of what God said and questions his Word. It's what the serpent did to Adam and Eve. It's what the devil did to Jesus (Matt 4:1–11; Mark 1:12–13; Luke 4:1–13). And it's what the Jerusalem Council was faced with in Acts 15. Some began teaching that circumcision was required for salvation. The council met and affirmed the truth that all are saved through the grace of Jesus. Nothing more was or is needed. In this way, they corrected the misinformation and held fast to the truth of the gospel.

A third telltale sign of misinformation is any teaching that diverts attention away from the Great Commission. The ultimate source of such teaching is the kingdom of darkness. Remember that Satan was disguised as an angel of light—a pseudo-minister of righteousness and an author of confusion in the church (1 Cor 14:33; 2 Cor 11:13–15). This happens so easily to us today in non-essential matters that turn our focus inward instead of to the harvest. For further treatment of this topic, consult *The Spiritual DNA of a Church on Mission Workbook*.

It's important to note that Satan's misinformation campaigns can also include a divide-and-conquer strategy. Even one degree of difference over time can cause a line to skew by many degrees. One degree of difference in doctrine can skew a believer and a church away from being fully aligned with God and his mission. Where did the teaching of compulsory circumcision come from in Acts 15? It came from believers! Scripture says it was men from Judea and later it was "some of the believers who belonged to the party of the Pharisees" (Acts 15:1, 5). We also see Paul warning the elders in Acts 20:30 that "Men will rise up even from your own number and distort the truth to lure the disciples into following them." Remain watchful for signs of division.

Misinformation campaigns can affect and disrupt the mission. In battle, there is something known as the fog of war. Decisions must be made based on accurate information. Prayer is a wartime weapon. John Piper wonderfully illustrates this. He says, "The number one reason prayer doesn't work for saints is because we have taken a wartime walkie-talkie and turned it into a domestic intercom."[8] A prayer covering is like a modern-day missile attack to knock out the anti-aircraft defenses, followed by an air assault taking out defensive positions in order to prepare the way for the ground troops

---

[8] John Piper, *Desiring God: Meditations of a Christian Hedonist*, rev. ed. (Colorado Springs: Multnomah, 2011), 177.

to take the enemy territory. People living on mission and especially those involved in church planting here and abroad are on the frontlines of the battle. It is critical that we believers stay immersed in Scripture and prayer so that we can stay true to the gospel.

Spiritual Warfare against the Demonic

The flagrant, demonic encounters in Ephesus represent a whole other level of spiritual warfare mostly foreign to us in North America. But we ought not to take lightly the power of the devil and his forces of darkness.

The church operates from the victory already won by Jesus Christ at Calvary. Paul reminds us in Romans that: "The God of peace will soon crush Satan under your feet (Rom 16:20a). Yes, we have victory in the present, but the beauty of this verse points forward to future victory as well. This promise hearkens all the way back to the garden when God said the "seed of woman" would crush the serpent (Gen 3:15). Jesus accomplished that mission when he cried out on the cross, "It is finished!" and the rest of this battle is for us to remain faithful to evangelize and make disciples for Christ.

Scripture teaches Satan is a fallen, created being who ultimately will be banished into hell (see Matt 25:41; Luke 10:18; Jude 6). Scripture also teaches the devil is not all-powerful, not all-knowing, and not all-present. He is absolutely unlike God, who is eternal in his existence, and who is all-powerful, all-knowing, and all-present. In stark contrast to Satan, God is all good, all loving, and all holy. In fact, even though Satan is like a roaring lion seeking whom he may devour, the book of Job tells us that he answers to God and cannot do anything more than the sovereign Lord allows (Job 1:1–22; 2:1–10).

In Ephesus, Paul performed "extraordinary miracles," including rebuking evil spirits who came out of people (Acts 19:11). But it wasn't until the seven sons of a Jewish high priest were overcome by a man controlled by a demon that fear came over the people and they held the name of the Lord in high esteem. Once that happened, believers began confessing their willing participation in the occult. They collected their magic books and destroyed them in a fire (Acts 19:19). This was a costly act as their value was exorbitant.

Any attempt to deal with the demonic in human strength will lead to grave consequences. Attempting to model what they had seen the missionaries do, the seven sons of Sceva (a Jewish chief priest) try to cast out a demon in their own strength. They assumed a formula would cast out demons like Paul by using the name of Jesus. Shockingly, the demon spoke to them, "I know Jesus, and I recognize Paul—but who are you?" The turn of events could best be described as a terrifying backfire for the seven sons. The evil spirit leaped on them, and they were sent running away naked and wounded in shame (Acts 19:13–17). Chuck Lawless writes:

> Spiritual warfare is not about learning a formula to overcome the enemy, it is instead about living a life that gives the enemy no place to get a foothold. Obedience, rather than ritual, overcomes the enemy.[9]

The spiritual DNA of spiritual warfare is available for activation in the battlefield for the one living the righteous life in Christ. This authority is only available for those who know the Lord Jesus and walk in obedience.

The story in Ephesus also warns us about objects. People today are inundated with a barrage of occult-based objects. We as believers can take too lightly the dark forces behind them, underestimating the bondage that can occur by dabbling in this realm. Such a list includes: deviant music, horror movies, Ouija boards, tarot cards, astrology, and witchcraft. These items become a gateway to darkness and entry into a spiritual quagmire. When we open ourselves to these kinds of objects, we invite the devil's activity into our life. It's imperative that these objects be avoided and destroyed.

The thief has declared war on you. He seeks to kill, steal, and destroy the abundant life within you (John 10:10). Just as mountain climbers need a foothold to move to another level on their ascent, the devil looks

---

[9] Lawless, *Disciple Warriors*, 214.

for footholds to drag you down into his evil descent. Think about the obvious footholds of the devil, starting with the paraphernalia of the occult world. In animistic cultures, people understand and even welcome the nature of the devil's footholds. These kinds of satanic footholds can render a person ineffective in God's mission while simultaneously working in the devil's favor.

When Paul later wrote to the church in Ephesus, he exhorted them not to give the devil a foothold. The idea is to not give the enemy an opportunity to gain influence (Eph 4:27). In addition to occult footholds by means of these objects, there are more subtle footholds we need to address.

The Foothold of Anger

Ephesians 4:26 says, "Be angry and do not sin." There is a righteous anger over sin that is acceptable for the believer, but Satan uses a *quick temper and a sinful angry spirit* to wreak havoc in many lives and churches. There is a healthy way to deal with anger and refrain from sinning. Do not let unrighteous anger become a foothold in your life and church because it will affect your missional effectiveness.

The Foothold of Security

The need for *security* is another common foothold. Scripture says, "The love of money is a root of all kinds of evil" (1 Tim 6:10). Seeing that their livelihood was at risk, a group of craftsmen incited a riot in Ephesus against Paul and the believers. The silversmiths wanted Paul and the believers out so they could continue profiting from sales of their statues of Artemis. In other words, the spread of the gospel impacted their pocketbooks (Acts 19:21–41). The enemy can gain a foothold in our lives over a love of money. It happened in Jerusalem with Ananias and Sapphira lying about their giving (Acts 5:1–11). It happened in Philippi when the fortune-teller was delivered from Satan's power (Acts 16:16–24). And it happened in Ephesus. Be on guard that it doesn't happen to you.

The Foothold of Withholding Forgiveness

Another common foothold is *withholding forgiveness*. It may be one of the tightest-gripping footholds the devil uses. Paul wrote 2 Corinthians in the context of offering forgiveness to someone who had grossly sinned against God and the church family. Paul said their "punishment" was sufficient and that they should "forgive and comfort him" so he was not "overwhelmed by excessive grief" (2 Cor 2:6–7). Why? Paul says, "so that we may not be taken advantage of by Satan" (2 Cor 2:11). It's nearly impossible to go into the harvest fields with a message of forgiveness when there's a strong foothold of unforgiveness in our hearts toward another person.

The Foothold of Confusion

Lastly, *confusion* is an effective foothold of the devil. In Ephesus, confusion ruled. Luke, describing the mood in the amphitheater, where Demetrius had gathered the people to incite them against Paul, wrote, "The assembly was in confusion, and most of them did not know why they had come together" (Acts 19:32). Later, Paul would write to the church in Corinth, who were dealing with confusion and disorder in their worship services as well as the teaching of false doctrines. Satan is the author of confusion and his objective is to rob us of God's peace and mission effectiveness (1 Cor 14:33).

How do we resist the footholds of the enemy? By pressing into the Lord in prayer, by immersing ourselves in the Word, and by opening our hearts to healing any place that isn't yielded to the Lord.

Spiritual Warfare against Infiltrators

Another strategy of the enemy is to infiltrate the ranks of believers with false teachers. As Paul prepared to depart Ephesus, he shed tears and warned the elders about false teachers (Acts 20:17–38). He had spent significant time pouring into these spiritual leaders and equipping them for ministry in God's Word. He warned them against "savage wolves" that would come from within, leading many astray, not sparing the flock. Jesus spoke of these infiltrators: "Be on your guard against false prophets who come to you in sheep's clothing but inwardly are ravaging wolves" (Matt 7:15). Paul described false teaching with the word *twisted*, which is exactly what Satan does with the Word of God.

Spiritual discernment is a dire need for believers today. False teachers have infiltrated the church, luring people away from God's mission of reaching a lost world with the gospel. Some positive feel-good preachers compromise the gospel and never take a stand for truth. Some are the legalistic mean-spirited preachers who push people away from the grace and freedom we have in Christ. Others preach with a cause other than the mission of God—it may be a social issue, a doctrinal focus, a new television station, a jet plane, or to pad their wallets. And still others preach a self-centered message masked as faith that God will give them everything their hearts' desire, especially material things.

Today, the pressing need in the church is to have true godly leaders who will propel God's people to be on mission for him. Beware of any false leader who points you away from the mission of God—a mission flowing with good fruit from a love relationship with the Lord Jesus. Be alert to the spiritual warfare surrounding you and the "leaders" you are following. From what Jesus said on the Sermon on the Mount, the mark of a true spiritual leader is a vital relationship with the Lord Jesus. He knows Christ personally, and in connection with him, produces good fruit. Religious activity and the appearance of spiritual warfare are not a measure of a relationship with the Lord. Rather, a spiritual person knows, seeks, and obeys God, and will push back the darkness every time (Matt 7:13–25).

Spiritual Warfare in the Modern Church

Risen Life Church in Salt Lake City reflects a church very much like Ephesus. They understand there is a spiritual reality that is more real than any physical reality human eyes can see. The church is a loving body of

Christ filled with grace and truth. Pastor Kevin Lund answered the call in 2008 to plant his life in Salt Lake City. The church holds a commitment to raising up the next generation of leaders and, to date, have planted two churches in the city.

Over the years, Pastor Kevin has experienced a good deal of spiritual warfare. He shares some helpful insights based on his experience: (1) "Spiritual warfare can best be characterized as mind games. It involves unexplainable torment and struggle with doubts. The devil is out to play you." (2) He reminds us there are three ways Christians are attacked as Paul taught the believers in Ephesus: the world, the passions of the flesh, and the prince of the power of the air (Eph 2:1–3). (3) He believes one of the tactics of the enemy is *isolation*. In essence, it's the idea of "hiding" or keeping up appearances and portraying perfection to others. He sees it all the time. The only things that counter hiding are healthy relationships and honest transparency in the life of the church.

How does Pastor Kevin combat spiritual warfare? The Word of God is the foundation of truth and will sustain us and our churches during demonic attacks. Pastor Kevin says, "The way to deal with widespread falsehoods is to know and apply the truth." For example, one false idea the devil actively promotes is that you will always be victorious and, if you struggle at all, there must be something wrong with your relationship with Christ. At Risen Life Church, they understand deeply that there is a price to be paid for following Christ in society. The battles, just as Paul shared with the Ephesians, are in the context of marriage, parenting, and work relationships. Robert Marshall, the teaching pastor, is quick to say, "We are opposed by a very strong enemy—strong compared to us but compared to God not strong at all."[10]

---

[10] Kevin Lund, pastor, Risen Life Church, interview with author, February 12, 2017; see his sermons on spiritual warfare at http://www.risenlifeutah.org/sermons.

Conclusion

As a young Anglican minister, John Wesley came to Christ upon hearing the gospel. He said, "My heart was strangely warmed." He was known for sharing the gospel, starting small groups, and enlisting an army of lay preachers who rode circuits on horseback preaching the gospel. Wesley expected spiritual warfare and opposition. In fact, when opposition was not present, Wesley would begin to question God's hand on his ministry. His great concern was that God had removed his hand.

One day he was riding his horse and realized three days had passed without an attack by the enemy. Immediately, he dismounted and fell to his knees, asking God to not remove his hand on his ministry. About that time an Anglican priest who despised Wesley saw him and began to throw rocks at him. Wesley leapt to his feet, raised his hands, and said, "Hallelujah! Thank you, Lord!"[11] We tend to think the absence of opposition is a good thing but we must understand the devil will fight us at every turn.

Satan is known as the accuser of the brothers and sisters in Christ (Rev 12:10). DNA evidence exonerated Richard Buckland and convicted the real perpetrator of those rapes and murders. DNA evidence became his advocate, just as Jesus Christ is the Advocate for every child of God who sins. He is the atoning sacrifice for us (1 John 2:1). Justice would have demanded the death penalty for all fallen, flawed humanity, but Jesus Christ paid the penalty by giving his life on the cross, living eternally to intercede for us now at the right hand of the Father. This is the storyline of victory in the spiritual war. While we're on mission with Jesus Christ, he has already won the war and continues to fight the battles on our behalf. Never forget: God always gets it right. Trust him, his Word, his ways, always remembering the truth that all things work together for the good of those who love him and are called according to his purpose. Be on mission with him.

---

[11] Rick Joyner, *The Morning Star Journal* (Fort Mill, SC: MorningStar Publications, 1996), 24.

Acts Immersion

Acts Action Item

Commit to fight the good fight of faith in your life and the life of your church.

Culture Change: Spiritual Warfare and Time

The devil knows his time is short and continues to work overtime. Do you recognize the time to be about God's mission is short? Hear the warning: "The devil has come down to you in great wrath because he knows that his time is short" (Rev 12:12). General Douglas McArthur provocatively said, "The history of failure in war can be summed up in two words: 'Too late!'"[12] This was the same man who famously said, "I shall return." McArthur had been forced to retreat from Taiwan in World War II and sometimes in the battle we need to retreat due to the devil's temptation. There is a time to stand and fight and a time to retreat to fight another day. Let's not be too late to enter the battle, but run with a godly sense of urgency to fight the good fight of faith and keep on fighting no matter the setback. Discernment is absolutely essential. Dedicate your time to be on mission. Jesus Christ promised to return soon, and the truth is when you look in the back of the book (the Bible), it clearly shows we win. Wherever you find yourself in the battle, always draw near to God because he has promised to draw near to you. Spiritual warfare ought to always draw us near to Jesus.

---

[12] Ed T. Imparato, *General MacArthur Speeches and Reports 1908–1964* (New York: Turner, 2000), 122.

Acts Character and Competence

Be...

- aware—of Satan's schemes, devices, and tactics against you
- vigilant—you are entering the enemy's territory to evangelize the lost, make disciples, and plant new churches
- dressed—with the full armor of God using both the offensive and the defensive weapons in Scripture (Eph 6:10–20)

Know...

- that spiritual warfare is real. There are no neutral zones or non-combatants
- that misinformation must be confronted with the truth
- that God has given spiritual authority and victory through the cross and resurrection
- that spiritual warfare overcomes the tactics of the devil, removing footholds and defeating strongholds (2 Cor 10:1–4)

Do...

- Prayerfully read the daily devotional "Acts Moment" and the Acts Bible readings below.
- Discern when to fight with the Word of God and prayer, and when to flee by running from temptation.
- Pledge your allegiance to Christ knowing the victory is already won.
- Commit to be at the corporate prayer time this week.

Acts Reading

Day 1: Acts 19:1–22
Day 2: Acts 19:23–41
Day 3: Acts 20:1–12
Day 4: Acts 20:13–38
Day 5: Acts 21:1–14

Acts Missionary Activity

Spiritual Warfare: Identify and Pray Against a Foothold

This week, identify a spiritual foothold or what some might call a stronghold in your life or community—a liquor store, a palm-reading establishment, a false doctrine, anger, confusion, or some other stronghold. Pray against it; ask God to do a mighty work of deliverance for those who own it, work in it, or exemplify it, as well as those who are influenced by it. If you've chosen one of the footholds, such as unforgiveness, take time to intercede for that person you know who may be harboring a grudge. Listen to what God may be saying about his using you to combat the darkness in its every form. Ask God to start a new church in the community that pushes back the darkness of the stronghold through the gospel. Ask God to use you to help someone deal with and remove a foothold in a person's life.

Reflection: Did you sense spiritual resistance as you prayed?

Spiritual Warfare in the Life of Christ

Jesus battled the devil and his dark forces throughout his ministry and life on mission. He clearly demonstrated how to overcome evil by relying on the Word of God, prayer, and the full armor of God.

For Further Reading

- *Disciple Warrior* by Church Lawless
- *The Devil Goes to Church* by Dave Butts
- *The Incredible Power of Kingdom Authority* by Adrian Rogers

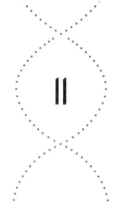

11

A Church in Action: Personalize the Spiritual DNA Principles

*Paul stayed two whole years in his own rented house.
And he welcomed all who visited him, proclaiming
the kingdom of God and teaching about the Lord Jesus
Christ with all boldness and without hindrance.*
—Acts 28:30–31

*Let's yearn for the Holy Spirit to write a story through us
that only his power can explain. I don't want my friends to
summarize my life as "The Acts of J. D. Greear." But the "Acts
of the Holy Spirit . . . through and around J. D. Greear."
He's writing his salvation project through me. And following
it as it unfolds has become the great adventure of my life.*
—J. D. Greear, *Jesus Continued*

DNA is one of the great discoveries of our generation, if not *the* greatest. Reconsider *Jurassic Park* when the voice-over from the trailer booms deeply, "The most phenomenal discovery of our time . . . becomes the greatest adventure of all time."[1] The novel and movie *Jurassic Park* is fictional, but God has been factually calling us to a phenomenal discovery and into the greatest adventure of all time through the book of Acts. It can be the defining mark of our lives if we choose to give ourselves to a greater story than Hollywood could ever write. Spiritual DNA discovery does indeed change everything!

Every person God uses has an Acts moment when they decide to courageously step up and obey the Lord. This decision changes the spiritual landscape of their own Jerusalem, Judea, Samaria, and ends of the earth. These kinds of people are like genetic engineers who reclaim their identity and call in Christ. The late beloved evangelism professor Roy Fish was one such man of God. He wrote:

> Every true believer desires to see the book of Acts replicated in our generation. The early believers did not have the educational opportunities and technological advances we have today. But they shook their world for Jesus Christ and spread His name across their known world. Our world needs to see Him presented again in a similar way. The multiplication of disciples and churches for the Lord Jesus is the way to achieve that objective.[2]

Did you catch Roy Fish's call to make the multiplication of disciples and churches the objective? Could it be that God places an innate desire within the spiritual DNA of every believer to see an Acts move of God in their generation? There are some who say if you don't learn from history, you're doomed to repeat it. But I say, and ask you to join me in saying, that the missional history of Acts is definitely worth repeating. These missional principles do not have an expiration date. I believe God has already made the

---

[1] "*Jurassic Park* (1993): Taglines, IMDb (Internet Movie Database), accessed September 25, 2017, http://www.imdb.com/title/tt0107290/taglines.

[2] Roy Fish, "The Great Commission: Making Disciples and Planting Churches," in *Reaching a Nation by Church Planting*, comp. Richard Harris, 2nd rev. (Alpharetta, GA: North American Mission Board SBC, 2005), 1.

way through giving his people the Holy Spirit and the spiritual DNA principles in Acts.

How do spiritual genetic engineers go about their task? First, they practically address mutations in their own life. They spend time in prayer and Scripture and make adjustments as the Holy Spirit leads. Second, they freely assist God's people in discovering their own missional potential in Christ. Alan Hirsch uses an excellent illustration in his book *The Forgotten Ways* from the beloved classic *The Wizard of Oz*. I'm sure you know the story but the outcome bears repeating in the context of this conclusion.

> But through all their ordeals and in their final victory they discover that in fact they already have what they were looking for—in fact they had it all along. The Scarecrow is very clever, the Tin Man has a real heart, and the Lion turns out to be very brave and courageous after all. They didn't need the Wizard at all. What they needed was a situation that forced them to discover, or activate, that which was already in them. They had what they were looking for, only they didn't realize it. To cap it off, Dorothy had her answer to her wish all along: she had the capacity to return home to Kansas—in her ruby slippers. By clicking them together three times, she is transported back to her home in Kansas.[3]

This journey back to Acts is intended to help us and our churches discover, rediscover, or activate these spiritual DNA principles through Christ—the missionary living within all of us. It is by walking out these principles in the mission field that we will discover our potential and see God move in mighty ways.

The Word of God is a living book. It is meant to be personalized. These "aha" moments when you see yourself in a verse or story can happen at any time. A memorable moment occurred for me during a training event for church planters. One of the participants was my friend, Japanese Pastor

---

[3] Alan Hirsch, *The Forgotten Ways: Reactivating Apostolic Movements* (Grand Rapids, MI: Baker, 2016), 8–9.

Kabari. God had called him to start a church in Chicago. He heard one of the trainers, Ed Handkins, speaking on the Great Commission. Ed emphatically repeated, "Jesus says, 'You go!' Jesus says, 'You go!'" Suddenly, my friend announced, "That's me . . . 'Yugo!'" Pastor Kabari's first name is Yugo. He verbalized and understood the mission of Jesus given to and embodied by those first disciples in Acts. Pastor Yugo joyfully made the personal connection. For decades, the church God used him to plant has been a gospel difference-maker for that community. It would help the cause of Christ if we would one and all personalize the book of Acts in our own lives. Begin by reading yourself into the story.

Figure 2
Spiritual Missionary DNA Double Helix Illustrated

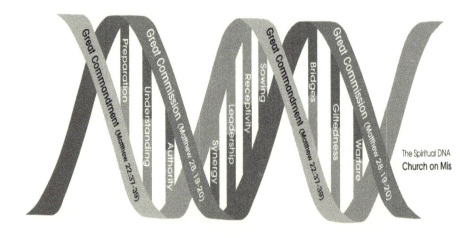

Personalized Solutions: Targeted Spiritual DNA Therapy

As a result of DNA discovery, medicical treatments are quickly moving to becoming more and more personalized. Dr. Randy Jirtle at Duke University recently helped launch the field of epigenetics. It is defined as the study of changes in organisms caused by modification of gene expression rather than alteration of the genetic code itself. Epigenetics has transformed the way we think about genomes. Through Dr. Jirtle's experiments with rats, he proved that unhealthy habits such as poor diet and lack of exercise can tag our DNA and cause cancer fighting cells to turn off, making us susceptible to cancer. In contrast, healthy habits such as good diet and exercise can turn on cancer fighting cells and change our life trajectory. These scientists are rewriting the rules of DNA because they discovered how to tell DNA to do specific things.[4] The promise of conquering many diseases with targeted and custom medicines will likely be readily available and commonplace in the future with DNA therapy.

Just as there are many actions we can take as individuals to make a difference in our personal health, there are steps we can take for the spiritual health of ourselves and our churches. For better or for worse, we do have a measure of control over our own genetic legacy and that of our churches. Is it possible to spiritually flip the DNA switch with targeted gene therapy? I've written this book with the conviction that it's entirely possible with God. When God's people decide to live like missionaries, the switch is flipped. Start with the book of Acts. Study it personally. Study it with your church. Dig deeply and prayerfully. Likely you are already excelling at some of the spiritual DNA strands. And likely there are some that need to be strengthened. As you study, God will give you a customized infusion, expression, and targeted application of his DNA. Then be ready to experience missional breakthrough because God always finds a way!

---

[4] Ethan Waters, "DNA Is Not Destiny: The New Science of Epigenetics," *Discover* magazine, November 22, 2006, http://discovermagazine.com/2006/nov/cover.

AFTERWORD
THE NEXT ACT FOR YOU AND YOUR CHURCH

The anemic condition of many churches is best described as complex and seemingly impossible to solve. The Rubik's Cube, a challenging puzzle, can give insight into God's solution for you and your church. Twisting the cube in random patterns will not work (especially with there being 43 quintillion combinations).[1] The more you try to fix it, the more it gets messed up, which is exactly what most of us do in church life. However, the Rubik's Cube puzzle can quickly be solved with access to the instruction book. The answer is provided in black and white on a page. Our instruction book, the Bible, does point the way for the life breaking free and God having his way in your life, your church, and the nation. Remember, physical DNA is compared to an instruction book. My aim has been to point you to the instructions in the Bible. Let us turn to the Gospels and the book of Acts, for it's there you'll find the biblical principles for missional revival. It's in black, white, and even red on the pages.

The Spiritual DNA of a Church on Mission is the anchor resource of an integrated pathway for you and your church to experience God and a missional revival that only he can bring. Without any doubt or hesitation, an immersion in Acts for an extended season and for reoccurring times in the

---

[1] Dan Harris, *Speed Solving the Cube: Easy-to-Follow, Step by Step Instructions for Many Popular 3-D Puzzles* (New York: Sterling, 1985), 18.

life of the church will positively affect the missional culture. My prayer has been that God will use this book to lead you to a greater knowledge and renewed appreciation of what a believer and a church on mission ought to look like. Because you've read it, I pray that God would impart to you a resolute attitude that every believer ought to live like a missionary and every church ought to be on mission. And it must begin first in you.

Most of all, I pray that God would give you a desire to experience missions firsthand by sharing the gospel, making disciples, ministering to those in need, and planting new churches among all peoples. Involvement in missions is the game changer that leads to Great Commission fulfillment. Think about it. If you only tell someone something, most likely he'll forget it. If you show someone something, he stands to remember it. However, involve him and the action is more likely to lead to an ongoing lifestyle change. This complete missional engagement must start with you and your people who are walking in the Holy Spirit and then spread throughout the entire body. Missional engagement is like the DNA of life itself . . . totally uncontained and unhindered. Then by God's grace, you and your church will be in a position to experience a book of Acts style missional revival and spiritual awakening in your spheres of influence.

Action Plan, Action Items, and the Book of Acts

To help you and your church on your journey, I created a companion resource titled *Spiritual DNA of a Church on Mission Workbook*. Before I introduce it to you, I'd like to begin with an admonition. My missionary mentor Chuck Lawless provides insight and wisdom to assist us with our expression of the spiritual DNA principles. He states the simple truth about revival: "It is the gift of God, and he grants it sovereignly according to his plan."[2] With

---

[2] Chuck Lawless, "Why the North America Church Is Unlikely to Experience Revival," *Chuck Lawless* (blog), December 7, 2018, http://chucklawless.com/2018/12/why-the-north-american-church-is-unlikely-to-experience-revival/.

that truth in mind, let us spiritually position ourselves to receive his gift and submit to his sovereign plan. Think about it. Historians have recorded and studied revivals and spiritual awakenings within North America. Not surprisingly so, the spiritual DNA principles in Acts can be traced within the accounts of those past powerful moves of God (see appendix 8 for a brief synopsis) which super excites me for you and your church.

The companion workbook is an operational guide to prepare your church for a God-given missional revival and a resource for further study (see appendix 1 for a preview of the table of contents). The heart and soul of the process is how to implement the seven cultural change factors in your life and the life of your church. The resource will help you lead your church into a time of mission plan and mission action by means of a church-wide revival, pathway, season, campaign, or whatever you choose to call it. Business author Laura Stack writes, "If the greatest enemy of action is the lack of a plan, the greatest enemy of a plan is the lack of action."[3] All these tools are aimed at immersion in the book of Acts for renewal and spiritual awakening individually, corporately, and, ultimately, overflowing onto your mission field to those who need to know Jesus Christ. The seven cultural change factors are:

1. Time Factor: Schedule Seasons of Repentance and Refreshing for Missions
2. Preaching Factor: Influence from the Pulpit for Missions
3. Praying Factor: Start the Church's Engine for Missions
4. Reading Factor: Hear and Apply the Word of God for Missions
5. Accountability Factor: Do Life Together in Christ for Missions
6. Leadership Factor: Mobilize Servant Leaders for Missions
7. Experience Factor: Provide On-the-Job Training for Missions

---

[3] Laura Stack, *Leave the Office Earlier: The Productivity Pro Shows You How to Do More in Less Time . . . and Feel Great About It* (New York: Random House, 2004), 11.

These factors provide a positive framework for how to lead your church to experience a rediscovery, application, and expression of the spiritual DNA from the first-century church.

This framework can be observed in Scripture, specifically in the story of Ezra. God's people set apart special times to seek him and dedicate their lives to serve him in fresh ways. Ezra is a testament that a correction in attitude and action precedes a transformed culture. All the cultural change factors for mission action emerge in this particular story line. You'll observe his spiritual leadership, the reading of the Scriptures, prayerful repentance, and proclamation of the Word. There was an accountability between the priests and people, an expectation of people's involvement, and, of course, special dedicated times before God (Ezra 1–10). God's transforming work came to his people because they met his conditions for renewal and refreshing. (The story of Josiah also possesses the same seven elements and factors—2 Kgs 22–23:30).

Orders Remain Unchanged

The missionary principles God has given us in Scripture apply to any time, context, culture, or circumstances. Warren Wiersbe affirms, "There are some non-repeatable events in Acts, as well as some transitional happenings; but the basic spiritual principles are the same today as when Peter and Paul ministered . . . if we will lay hold of the "power principles" recorded in Acts, we can be dynamic and see our local churches do exploits for the Lord."[4] Do words like *power*, *dynamic*, and *exploits* (daring and heroic acts) describe you and your church? The first-century believers acted in obedience to the Great Commission and were empowered with the Holy Spirit for faithful mission action.

While visiting Washington D.C., our family went to observe the changing of the guard at Arlington Cemetery where the Tomb of the Unknown

---

[4] Warren W. Wiersbe, *Be Dynamic: Experience the Power of God's People—Acts 1–12* (Colorado Springs: David C. Cook, 1987), 15.

Soldier is prominently located. With impeccable, faithful duty, the tomb is guarded around the clock and in all weather conditions. A regular changing of the guard occurs at various intervals. At each change, the guard leaving his post relays to the other guard, "Orders remain unchanged."

The same powerful word is true for us and our churches on mission. Our marching orders found in the words of Jesus and the book of Acts have not changed from the first century: "Go, therefore, and make disciples of all nations, baptizing them in the name of the Father and of the Son and of the Holy Spirit, teaching them to observe everything I have commanded you. And remember, I am with you always, to the end of the age" (Matt 28:19–20).

The orders remain unchanged.

APPENDIX I
PREVIEW OF *THE SPIRITUAL DNA OF A CHURCH ON MISSION WORKBOOK: CHURCH GENOME PROJECT*

Contents

Introduction: One Pivotal Story
Chapter 1. Time Factor
Chapter 2. Preaching Factor
Chapter 3. Praying Factor
Chapter 4. Reading Factor
Chapter 5. Experience Factor
Chapter 6. Accountability Factor
Chapter 7. Leadership Factor
Conclusion: An Equipping Center for Missional Engagement
Church Genome Project: Participant's Resource Hub
Church Genome Project: Be a Missional Culture Change Agent for Christ
Church Genome Project: Next Missional Steps for Church Planting Involvement
Church Genome Project: Five Spiritual DNA Couplets: Revitalization
Church Genome Project: Pastor's Resource Hub
Afterword

APPENDIX 2
THE SPIRITUAL DNA PRINCIPLES IN THE CHURCHES OF ACTS

Principle	Expression	Illustrative Church Plant
Spiritual Preparation	Wait, Pray, and Expect God to Work	Jerusalem *Acts 1:1–2:1*
Spiritual Authority	Rely on the Holy Spirit's Power	Jerusalem *Acts 2:1–8:1*
Spiritual Understanding	Focus on Peoples and Places	Jerusalem, Caesarea *Acts 2:5–13; 11:1*
Spiritual Leadership	Identify and Nurture Missional Leaders	Antioch *Acts 11:19–30; Acts 13:1–4*
Spiritual Synergy	Work Together for Greater Impact	Philippi *Acts 16:1–40*
Spiritual Receptivity	Find the People of Peace	Philippi *Acts 16:6–40*
Spiritual Sowing	Evangelize and Make Disciples	Thessalonica/Berea *Acts 17:1–15*
Spiritual Bridges	Leverage Points of Connection	Athens *Acts 17:16–34*

Spiritual Giftedness	Gather and Give Resources from the Harvest	Corinth *Acts 18:1–18*
Spiritual Warfare	Fight the Good Fight of Faith	Ephesus *Acts 19:1–41; 20:13–38*

APPENDIX 3
THE SPIRITUAL DNA PRINCIPLES IN THE LIFE OF CHRIST

Principle	Expression	An Example in Jesus's Life
Spiritual Preparation	Wait, Pray, and Expect God to Work	Jesus prepared his disciples *Matthew 10, Luke 10*
Spiritual Authority	Rely on the Holy Spirit's Power	Jesus relied on Holy Spirit *Luke 4:18–19*
Spiritual Understanding	Focus on Peoples and Places	Jesus engaged Samaritans *John 4:1–26*
Spiritual Leadership	Identify and Nurture Missional Leaders	Jesus led by serving others *John 13:1–19*
Spiritual Synergy	Work Together for Greater Impact	Jesus formed his team *Mark 3:16–19*
Spiritual Receptivity	Find the People of Peace	Jesus delivered the demoniac *Mark 5:19; 53–56*
Spiritual Sowing	Evangelize and Make Disciples	Jesus preached gospel *Matt 4:17; Luke 5:10*
Spiritual Bridges	Leverage Points of Connection	Jesus taught in parables *Matt 13:11–16*

Spiritual Giftedness	Gather and Give Resources from the Harvest	Jesus fed the multitudes *John 6:1–15*
Spiritual Warfare	Fight the Good Fight of Faith	Jesus overcame the devil *Matthew 4; Luke 4*

APPENDIX 4
THE SPIRITUAL DNA PRINCIPLES IN THE MISSIONARY DISCOURSES

Principle	Expression	Missionary Discourses
Spiritual Preparation	Wait, Pray, and Expect God to Work	*Matt 10:5, 9–10* *Luke 10:2–24* *Mark 6:8–11*
Spiritual Authority	Rely on the Holy Spirit's Power	*Matt 10:1, 17–20* *Luke 10:1–3* *Mark 6:7*
Spiritual Understanding	Focus on Peoples and Places	*Matt 9:35–37; 10:6* *Luke 10:1, 13–15, 21* *Mark 6:6*
Spiritual Leadership	Identify and Nurture Missional Leaders	*Matt 9:37; 10:2–4* *Luke 10:1, 17* *Mark 6:7*
Spiritual Synergy	Work Together for Greater Impact	*Matt 10:2–4* *Luke 10:1* *Mark 6:7*

Spiritual Receptivity	Find the People of Peace	*Matt 10:11–16, 40*
		Luke 10:5–16
		Mark 6:10–11
Spiritual Sowing	Evangelize and Make Disciples	*Matt 10:8*
		Luke 10:9–11
		Mark 6:12
Spiritual Bridges	Leverage Points of Connection	*Matt 10:11, 42*
		Luke 10:5–8
		Mark 6:10
Spiritual Giftedness	Gather and Give Resources from the Harvest	*Matt 9:37, 10:8*
		Luke 10:2–4
		Mark 6:13
Spiritual Warfare	Fight the Good Fight of Faith	*Matt 10:17–23; 34–39*
		Luke 10:3, 16–20
		Mark 6:7, 13

APPENDIX 5
THE SPIRITUAL DNA PRINCIPLES AS MODERN MUTATIONS

Principle	Modern Mutation Expression	Biblical Response
Spiritual Preparation	Impatient, Self-Sufficent, and Doubtful	*Yield to God's next steps* *Rom 12:1–2; 2 Cor 12:9*
Spiritual Authority	Autocratic, Self-Reliant, and Powerless	*Rely on Christ and his Spirit* *John 15:5; 1 Cor 12:3*
Spiritual Understanding	Exclusive, Prejudicial, and Racist	*Reach out to all peoples* *Rom 1:16; Gal 3:26–29*
Spiritual Leadership	Insecure, Entitled, and Immobilized	*Be an equipper of the saints* *1 Cor 15:9–10; Eph 4:11–16*
Spiritual Synergy	Individualistic, Uncooperative, and Divisive	*Work together with God* *Col 3:14; 1 Cor 3:5–9*
Spiritual Receptivity	Non-strategic, Unintentional, and Marketer	*Leverage receptive peoples* *Rom 15:18–21; 2 Thess 3:1*

Spiritual Sowing	Failure to Prioritize Evangelism and Discipleship	*Do the work of the evangelist and a disciple-maker Matt 28:19–20; 2 Tim 4:5*
Spiritual Bridges	Full Embrace or Failure to Engage Culture	*Be culturally relevant and true to the gospel message 1 Cor 9:19–23; 1 John 2:15*
Spiritual Giftedness	Abuse of Gifts and Consumer-Oriented	*Do all things in love 1 Cor 12–14; Gal 6:1–10*
Spiritual Warfare	Obsession or Avoidance of Warfare	*Put on armor of God 2 Cor 10:1–6; Eph 6:1–10*

APPENDIX 6
THE SPIRITUAL DNA PRINCIPLES IN THE CHURCH AT PHILIPPI (MICRO VIEW)

Principle	Expression	Scripture References
Spiritual Preparation	Wait, Pray, and Expect God to Work	Acts 16:6–9
Spiritual Authority	Rely on the Holy Spirit's Power	Acts 16:6–10
Spiritual Understanding	Focus on Peoples and Places	Acts 16:10–12
Spiritual Leadership	Identify and Nurture Missional Leaders	Acts 16:13–15
Spiritual Synergy	Work Together for Greater Impact	Acts 16:10, 19
Spiritual Receptivity	Find the People of Peace	Acts 16:14, 27–34
Spiritual Sowing	Evangelize and Make Disciples	Acts 16:14, 31

Spiritual Bridges	Leverage Points of Connection	*Acts 16:13, 16*
Spiritual Giftedness	Gather and Give Resources from the Harvest	*Acts 16:34*
Spiritual Warfare	Fight the Good Fight of Faith	*Acts 16:16–18, 22–25*

APPENDIX 7
THE SPIRITUAL DNA PRINCIPLES IN THE PARABLES

1. Spiritual Preparation:
   - Two Houses (Matt 7:21–28)
   - Ten Virgins (Matt 25:1–13)
   - Barren Fig Tree Nurtured (Luke 13:6–9)
   - Tower Builder and King to War (Luke 14:25–32)
   - Unrighteous Judge and Widow (Luke 18:1–8)

2. Spiritual Authority:
   - Friend at Midnight (Luke 11:5–13)
   - Rock and Keys (Matt 16:15–19)
   - Coin with Caesar's Inscription (Matt 20:20–26)

3. Spiritual Understanding
   - Mustard Seed (Matt 13:31–32)
   - Good Samaritan (Luke 10:30–37)
   - Puppies and Crumbs (Matt 15:21–28)

4. Spiritual Leadership
   - Yoke and Burden (Matt 11:28–30)
   - Leaven in Three Measures of Dough (Matt 13:33–35)
   - Blind Leaders (Matt 15:14)

- Two Sons and Vineyard (Matt 21:28–32)
- Duty of Leaders (Luke 17:1–10)

5. Spiritual Synergy
   - Dragnet—Fishers of Men (Matt 4:19; Matt 13:37–50)
   - Vineyard Workers (Matt 20:1–16)
   - Light and Basket (Mark 4:21–25)

6. Spiritual Receptivity
   - Dogs and Swine (Matt 7:6)
   - Generation and Children (Matt 11:16–17)
   - Sower and Soils (Matt 13:1–23)
   - Invitations to Banquet (Luke 14:15–24)

7. Spiritual Sowing
   - Sower and Soils (Matt 13:1–23)
   - Mustard Seed (Matt 13:31–32)
   - Narrow and Broad Gate (Matt 7:12–14)
   - Growing Seed (Mark 4:26–29)
   - Lost Sheep, Coin, and Son (Luke 15:1–32)
   - Rich Man and Lazarus (Luke 16:19–31)

8. Spiritual Bridges
   - Salt and Light (Matt 5:13–16)
   - Patches and New Wineskins (Matt 9:16–17)
   - Treasure Hidden and Pearl of Great Price (Matt 13:44–46)
   - Jonah and Queen (Matt 12:38–42)
   - Gnat and Camel (Matt 23:24)
   - Shrewd Dishonest Manager (Luke 16:1–13)

9. Spiritual Giftedness
   - Treasures in Heaven (Matt 6:19–20)
   - Scribe and Householder (Matt 13:51–52)
   - Talents (Matt 25:14–30)

- Sheep and Goats (Matt 25:31–46)
- Rich Fool and His Barns (Mark 12:13–21)

10. Spiritual Warfare
    - Sheep and Wolves (Matt 7:15)
    - Empty House and Unclean Spirits (Matt 12:43–45)
    - Tares and Wheat (Matt 13:24–30; 36–43)
    - House Divided and Unclean Spirits (Luke 11:14–26)
    - King Going to War (Luke 14:31–32)

APPENDIX 8
THE SPIRITUAL DNA PRINCIPLES IN AWAKENINGS AND REVIVALS OF NORTH AMERICA

Church Planting Principle	Example(s) from Awakenings and Revivals
Spiritual Preparation	Jonathan Edwards: a call to prayer for a revival of religion (First Great Awakening, 1734–1770)
Spiritual Authority	Henry Blackaby: Saskatoon revivals, with a fresh discovery of God's activity through the Word of God and the Holy Spirit (1971)
Spiritual Understanding	David Brainerd: focus on peoples in his mission work with Native Americans (First Great Awakening, 1734–1770)
Spiritual Leadership	Shubal Stearns: Sandy Creek Baptist Church: identified and nurtured leaders from within this mother, grandmother, and great-grandmother church (Church Planting Movement, 1755–1772)

Spiritual Synergy	George Whitefield and Gilbert Tennent: the effective team working together to conduct evangelistic gatherings (First Great Awakening, 1734–1770)
Spiritual Receptivity	John Wesley: the practice of discovering people of peace among the homesteaders and the use of circuit rider preachers (First Great Awakening, 1734–1770)
Spiritual Sowing	D. L. Moody: a renewed passion for lost souls, gospel proclamation, and making disciples (revivals through his ministry 1860–1899)
Spiritual Bridges	Jeremiah Lanphier: the gospel penetrated the marketplace through the Businessman's Prayer Revival beginning in New York City (1857–1859)
Spiritual Giftedness	Samuel Mills and friends: the famous Haystack Revival, which God used to mobilize college students for a global missionary movement (Second Great Awakening, 1787–1843)
Spiritual Warfare	James McGready: the western camp meetings of Kentucky and their willingness to enter into "Rogues Harbor" with the gospel in spite of fierce opposition (Second Great Awakening, 1787–1843)

*Sources

Malcolm McDow and Alvin L. Reid, *Firefall: How God Has Shaped History Through Revivals*

Henry T. Blackaby and Claude V. King, *Experiencing God: Knowing and Doing the Will of God*

APPENDIX 9
THE SPIRITUAL DNA PRINCIPLES IN ENTREPRENEURSHIP

Church Planting Principle	Entrepreneurial Principles
Spiritual Preparation	Business Plan and Systems Design
Spiritual Authority	Empowerment and Branding
Spiritual Understanding	Vision, Mission, and Communication
Spiritual Leadership	Leadership Development and Delegation
Spiritual Synergy	Teamwork, Volunteerism, and Alignment
Spiritual Receptivity	Market and Customer Research
Spiritual Sowing	Sales Prospecting and Communication
Spiritual Bridges	Marketing and Networking
Spiritual Giftedness	Productivity, Venture Capital, and Volunteers
Spiritual Warfare	Courage, Risk, and Conflict Resolution

ABOUT THE AUTHOR

Bob Burton and his wife, Dana, have been married since 1989. They have three married sons and two grandchildren. Bob has served as a church planter, pastor, and on church staff prior to joining the North American Mission Board in 2001. He serves the churches of the Send Network through the Multiplication Pipeline Team. He has earned his master of religious education from Midwestern Baptist Theological Seminary and his doctor of educational leadership from The Southern Baptist Theological Seminary. His passion is to see pastors and churches discover their next missional step for God's glory—helping to move people from pews to action.

NAME AND SUBJECT INDEX

A
Abraham waiting, 13
accountability, 32
Acts Spectrum, 6
affinities, 45
Agrippa (king), 105
Akin, Daniel, 113
Allen, Roland, 8
Allmond, Joy, 99
Anderson, Alaric, 112
Anderson, Justin, 56
Anderson, Neil T., 149
Andrews, Scott, xvii
Apollos, 136, 150
armor of God, 149
Augustine of Hippo, 18

B
Baker, Robert, 54
Balmer, Randall H., 119
Barnabas, 58, 131
basic training (Army), 20
Bird, Warren, 69
bivocational tentmakers, 138
Blackaby, Henry T., xv, 11, 18, 98
Blackaby, Richard, 98
Blanchard, Ken, 71
Bock, Darrell L., 115
Boyles, Salynn, 108
Brengle, Samuel Logan, 59
Bruce, F. F., 10, 58, 70, 104

Buckland, Richard, 146, 158
Burgin, Jim, 88
Burgin, Tillie, 88
Burton, Bob, 70
Butts, David, 147

C
Carey, William, 9, 10
Cathcart, William, 54
Cathy, Truett, 64
centurion, 26
cessation, 6
character, 58
Chester, Tim, 138
Chesterton, G. K., 137
Choi, David, 17–18
Christopherson, Jeff, 28, 98
cities, 44
Clifton, Clint, 34
Clifton, Mark, 55
cloning, 62
Cobain, Ian, 145
Cole, Neil, 83
Collins, Jim, 64
Comer, Gary, 121
Comfort, Ray, 117
compatibility, 60
contextualization, 114
Cook, Keelan, 113
Cordeiro, Wayne, 73, 74
Cornelius, 40

Crichton, Michael, 2, 7
Crispus, 136

D
David, leadership, 63
demonic, 152–53
Deryugina, Natalia, 123
discernment, 156
disciple making, 98–99
DNA
    definition, 20
    metaphor, xvii
    profiling, 145–55
    test, 127–28
Drucker, Peter, 64
Dvorsky, George, 68
Dwight, Sereno, 15
Dyrness, William, 102

E
Ebert, Mike, 105
Eberwine, James, 142
Edwards, Jonathan, 15
Engel, James, 102
Engel Scale, 102
Engstrom, Todd, 75
entropy, 69
environment versus experience, 79–80
Epicureans, 115
epigenetics, 167
Eulerian Path, 122
evangelism, 71
evolution, 2, 117
Ezell, Kevin, 105

F
Fernando, Ajith, 31
Fish, Roy, 164
Fitt, Arthur Percy, 44
fivefold offices, 133
footholds, 154–55
Forrester, Duncan B., 137
Frost, Robert, xi
fruit of gospel seed, 99
Frye, Bryan, 120

G
Galli, Mark, 50, 103
Garrison, David, 41
general revelation, 117
Golden Circle, xvi
good Samaritan, 139
gospel conversations, 105
Graham, Billy, 12, 119
Graph Theory, 122
Great Awakening, 15
Great Commission, 42
Greear, J. D., 61, 104
Greenleaf, Robert K., 64
Green, Michael, 35
Greeson, Kevin, 115
Grudem, Wayne A., 7

H
Hamer, Dean H., 80
Hanson, Joe, 2
Harris, Dan, 169
Harris, Nadine Burke, 142
Harris, Richard, 164
Hartwig, Ryan, 69
Havner, Vance, 4
Hearn, Mark, 42
heart language, 39
hedonism, 115
Hermes and Zeus, 150
Hillman, Os, 119
hindrances, 6
Hirsch, Alan, 165
holiness, 113
Holy Spirit
    authority, 25
    baptism, 30
    filling, 30–31
    missions, 32
Hybels, Bill, 57

I
idols, 116
immigrants, 43
Imparato, Ed T., 159
intelligent design, 117
international students, 43

J

James, Stuart H., 145
Jeffreys, Alec, 145
Jerusalem Council, 150–52
Jerusalem population, 10
Jesus's leadership, 56
Jesus's missionary discourses, 91
Jirtle, Dr. Randy, 166
Joyner, Rick, 158
Jurassic Park, 1–2, 7, 163–64

K

Kimbrough, S. T., 81
Kingdom catalyst, 28
Kingdom maximizers, 83
kingdom of God, 15, 96

L

Lake, Mac, 28, 98
Lanphier, Jeremiah, 119
Larson, Gary, 148
Lawless, Chuck E., 149, 153, 170
leadership, defined, 53
Level 5 Leaders, 64
Lewis, C. S., 26
Lund, Kevin, 157
Lycaonians, 112

M

Mabilog, Patrick, 116
MacMillan, Pat, 69
man of the tombs, 86
marketplace ministry, 119
Mathis, Erma H., 88
Mayes, Gary, 27, 90
McArthur, Douglas, 159
McGavran, Donald, 91
McGee, J. Vernon, 5
McHenry, Raymond, 49
Means, Howard, 96
military, 33–34
miracles, 120
missional community, 75
missional preaching, 108
mission, missions, and missional, 3
Moody, Paul Dwight, 44

moralism, 115–16
multiethnic church, 42
multi-housing ministry, 88
Muslims, 115
mutations, 69
Mylander, Charles, 149

N

Nall, Brian, 140
nations, 42
nature versus nurture, 53–54
Newport, Kenneth G. C., 81
Nordby, Jon J., 145
Norman, R. Stanton, 113

O

obedience, 56, 90
Oikos households, 84
Olson, Dan, 141
optics, 140
Orr, J. Edwin, 16

P

Pachkovskaya, Yana, 123
Packer, J. I., 36
Pentecost, 12
people groups, 41
Perry, Tobin, 17
person of peace, 83
persuasion, 104
Pethers, Dennis, 102
Pierson, A. T., 16
Piper, John, 151
Platt, David, 137
Ponder, Lynn, 18
prayer in missions, 11
Prayer Meeting Revival, 119
prayer of Jesus, 16–17
preaching evangelistically, 104
Putman, Jim, 106

R

receptive peoples/places, 91
refugees, 43
Reid, Alvin, 107
relational networks, 84

resources in the harvest, 131
resurrection, 117
revival conditions, 12
Roberson, A. T., 72
Roberts, Bob, 50
Robinson, Tara Rodden, 26
Rogers, Adrian, 121
Rubik's Cube, 169

S

Sanders, Van, 41
Sandy Creek, 54–55
Satan, 152
Schaeffer, Francis A., 118, 146
Schwarz, Christian, 97
science, 117
Send North America, 44
servant leaders, 56, 64
Shearer, John, 59
signs and wonders, 119–20
Sinek, Simon, xvi
Slaughter, Michael, 62
Smith, Ebbie, 56
Smith, E. Elbert, 82
soul whisper, 121
sovereignty of God, 117, 170
special revelation, 136
spiritual gifts, 130
    list of, 132–133
spontaneous expansion, 7–8
Spurgeon, Charles H., 99
Stack, Laura, 171
Stearns, Shubal, 54
Stephen (martyr), 13
Stetzer, Ed, 113
Stoics, 115
Stott, John R. W., 44, 100
stuttering genes, 108
sufficiency of God, 117
synagogue, 42

synergy, 67

T

talents, 138–139
targeted gene therapy, 167
tax collectors, 46
teams, dysfunctional, 69
teamwork, 69
temptations of Christ, 147–48
Terry, John Mark, 56
Teykel, Terry, 18
time, 134–135
Titius Justus, 136
Tizon, Al, 109
Towns, Elmer, 147
trauma-informed learning, 142
treasures, 136–137
Tyson, Neil deGrasse, 116

U

university students, 120
unknown God, 48, 114

V

Vance, Mark, 120
Vine, W. E., 101, 102, 103, 104, 114

W

Wagner, C. Peter, 106
Waters, Ethan, 167
Waule, K., 112
Wiersbe, Warren W., 172
Wilkes, C. Gene, 56
Willis, Jr., Avery T., 11, 18
will of God, 70–71
Winter, Ralph D., 41
witness, 30
Wolf, Thomas A., 84
woman at the well, 85
Wuest, Kenneth Samuel, 29

SCRIPTURE INDEX

Genesis
3:15 *152*
12:4 *13*
21:4 *13*
37:2 *13*
41:46 *13*

Exodus
3 *108*
33:11–23 *17*

Deuteronomy
28:1–2 *12*

1 Samuel
20:1–42 *62*

2 Samuel
23:8–39 *62*

2 Kings
22–23:30 *172*

2 Chronicles
7:14 *12*

Ezra
1–10 *172*

Job
1:1–22 *152*
2:1–10 *152*

Psalms
19:1 *116*
46:10 *48*
78:70–72 *62*
96:7–9 *xiii*
105:17–22 *13*
126:5–6 *95*
139:14 *116*

Ecclesiastes
4:9–12 *74*

Isaiah
55:11 *110*

Joel
2:12–14 *13*
2:28–32 *31*

Matthew
4 *180*
4:1–11 *150*
4:3 *147*
4:9 *147*
4:17 *97, 179*
4:19 *99, 188*
5:13–16 *188*
6:19–20 *188*
7:6 *188*
7:12–14 *188*
7:13–25 *156*
7:15 *156, 189*

7:21–28 *187*
8:5–13 *26*
8:9 *26*
9:16–17 *188*
9:35–37 *181*
9:36 *49*
9:37 *181, 182*
10 *91, 179*
10:1 *27, 181*
10:2–4 *181*
10:5 *181*
10:6 *42, 181*
10:8 *182*
10:8b *131*
10:9–10 *181*
10:11 *182*
10:11–16 *182*
10:14 *82, 135*
10:17–20 *181*
10:17–23 *182*
10:19–20 *28, 38*
10:34–39 *182*
10:40 *182*
10:40–42 *131*
10:42 *182*
11:16–17 *188*
11:28–30 *187*
12:38–42 *188*
12:43–45 *189*
13:1–23 *188*
13:11–16 *179*
13:24–30 *189*
13:31–32 *187, 188*
13:33–35 *187*
13:36–43 *189*
13:37–50 *188*
13:44–46 *188*
13:51–52 *188*
15:14 *187*
15:21–28 *187*
16:15–19 *187*
18:19–20 *150*
20:1–16 *188*
20:20–26 *187*
20:25–28 *64*
21:28–32 *188*
23:24 *188*

25:1–13 *187*
25:14–30 *139, 188*
25:21 *139*
25:31–46 *189*
25:41 *152*
27:40 *147*
28:18 *25, 27*
28:18–20 *27*
28:19–20 *31, 173, 184*
28:20 *136*
28:20b *27*

Mark

1:12–13 *150*
2:1–12 *47*
3:13–18 *68*
3:14 *29*
3:16–19 *179*
4:21–25 *188*
4:26–27 *96*
4:26–29 *188*
5:1–20 *86*
5:19 *86, 179*
5:53–56 *179*
6:6 *181*
6:7 *27, 68, 181, 182*
6:7–13 *91*
6:8–11 *181*
6:10 *182*
6:10–11 *182*
6:11 *82, 135*
6:12 *182*
6:13 *182*
6:53–56 *86*
10:45 *56*
11:22 *148*
12:13–21 *189*

Luke

4 *180*
4:1–13 *150*
4:18–19 *179*
5:10 *179*
5:29 *46*
7:34 *46*
9:5 *82*
10 *179*

Scripture Index

10:1 *27, 68, 181*
10:1–3 *181*
10:1–24 *91*
10:2-4 *182*
10:2–24 *181*
10:3 *182*
10:5–6 *79*
10:5–8 *182*
10:5–16 *182*
10:7 *131*
10:9–11 *182*
10:11 *82*
10:13–15 *181*
10:16 *88*
10:16–20 *182*
10:17 *181*
10:18 *152*
10:21 *181*
10:30–37 *187*
10:32 *13*
11:5–13 *187*
11:14–26 *189*
13:6–9 *187*
14:15–24 *188*
14:25–32 *187*
14:31–32 *189*
15:1–2 *46*
15:1–32 *188*
16:1–13 *188*
16:19–31 *188*
17:1–10 *188*
17:21 *15*
18:1–8 *187*
19:1 10 *15, 46*
22:42 *55*
24:48–49 *9*
24:49 *10*

John

3:16 *89*
4 *85*
4:1–26 *179*
5:19–20 *84*
6:1–15 *180*
10:10 *153*
10:27 *48*
12:24 *97*

13:1–19 *179*
14:11 *120*
15:5 *183*
17:11 *123*
17:20–23 *17*
20:21 *27*

Acts

1 *5, 11*
1:1 *4*
1:1–2:1 *177*
1:1–11 *22*
1:3 *15, 103*
1:4–5 *13*
1:5 *30*
1:6 *29*
1:7–8 *27*
1:8 *xv, 29, 30, 35, 37, 150*
1:12–26 *22*
2 *11*
2:1–8:1 *177*
2:1–13 *22*
2:5–13 *177*
2:14–41 *22*
2:16–21 *31*
2:32 *104*
2:40 *107*
2:42–47 *22*
2:43 *104*
3:1–10 *37*
3:6 *141*
3:11–26 *37*
3:15 *104*
4:1 *22, 37*
4:23–31 *37*
4:32–37 *37, 138*
4:42–47 *32*
5:1–11 *32, 51, 154*
5:3 *32*
5:9 *32*
5:12–16 *51*
5:17–42 *52*
5:32 *104*
6 *14*
6:1–7 *32, 52, 138*
6:8–15 *52*
7 *99*

7:1–8 *13*
7:1–53 *66*
7:6–7 *13*
7:9–16 *13*
7:17–50 *13*
7:30 *13*
7:36 *13*
7:54–8:3 *66*
8 *47*
8:4–8:8 *66*
8:9–25 *32, 66*
8:26–40 *66*
8:30–31 *101*
9:1–19 *77*
9:20–31 *77*
9:26–31 *58*
9:32–43 *77*
10 *40, 47*
10:1 *41*
10:1–8 *77*
10:9–23 *77*
10:23–48 *93*
10:39 *104*
10:44 *40*
11:1 *177*
11:1–18 *93*
11:19–21 *57, 107*
11:19–30 *93, 177*
11:21 *56*
11:24 *56*
11:25–26 *59*
11:26 *28, 58*
11:27–30 *138*
11:30 *59*
12:1–19 *93*
12:20–25 *93*
13 *14*
13:1–3 *110*
13:1–4 *177*
13:2 *57*
13:4–12 *110*
13:8–20 *150*
13:13 *58*
13:13–52 *110*
13:16–41 *112*
13:31 *104*

13:46 *58*
13:50 *58*
13:51 *82*
14:1–20 *110*
14:8–18 *112*
14:21–22 *82*
14:21–28 *110*
15 *32, 150, 151*
15:1 *151*
15:1–35 *124*
15:5 *151*
15:25–26 *58*
15:36–41 *59, 124*
16 *14, 47, 70, 82, 83, 85*
16:1–5 *124*
16:1–10 *70*
16:1–40 *177*
16:6–9 *185*
16:6–10 *124, 185*
16:6–13 *82*
16:6–34 *70*
16:6–40 *177*
16:9 *84*
16:10 *70, 71, 185*
16:10–12 *185*
16:11–40 *124*
16:13 *186*
16:13–14 *11*
16:13–15 *185*
16:14 *84, 185*
16:14–15 *83*
16:14–31 *82*
16:15 *84*
16:16 *11, 186*
16:16–18 *186*
16:16–24 *154*
16:16–34 *72*
16:19 *185*
16:22–25 *186*
16:25 *11*
16:27–34 *185*
16:28 *87*
16:31 *84, 185*
16:32–34 *82*
16:32–40 *87*
16:34 *186*

16:35–40 *82*
16:40 *82*
17 *48*
17:1–2 *99*
17:1–9 *144*
17:1–15 *97, 177*
17:2 *80, 101*
17:2–6 *98*
17:3 *101*
17:5–9 *103*
17:6 *98, 100*
17:10–12 *100*
17:10–15 *144*
17:14–16 *114*
17:15–34 *112*
17:16 *114*
17:16–34 *144, 177*
17:23 *48, 111*
17:24–29 *117*
17:25 *117*
17:26–27 *39, 42*
17:28 *117, 118*
17:34 *121*
18:1–10 *134*
18:1–17 *134, 144*
18:1–18 *178*
18:2 *134*
18:5 *138*
18:6 *135*
18:7 *136*
18:9–10 *135*
18:10–11 *136*
18:11 *135*
18:18–28 *144*
18:20 28 *146*
18:24–28 *136, 150*
19:1–4 *146*
19:1–7 *150*
19:1–22 *160*
19:1–41 *178*
19:11 *152*
19:13–17 *153*
19:19 *153*
19:21–41 *154*
19:23–41 *160*
19:32 *155*

20:1–12 *160*
20:5–21:17 *70*
20:13–38 *160, 178*
20:17–38 *146, 155*
20:30 *151*
20:33–35 *138*
21:1–14 *160*
22:15 *104*
26 *105*
27:1–28:16 *70*
28 *105*
28:28 *105*
28:30–31 *163*
28:31 *15*

Romans

1:16 *42, 183*
4:16–25 *13*
8:9–11 *34*
8:28 *87*
10:17 *104*
12:1–2 *183*
12:6–8 *133*
12:8 *60*
12:13 *138*
15:4 *1*
15:18–21 *183*
16:1–27 *72*
16:3–5a *136*
16:20a *152*

1 Corinthians

1:18 *104*
3:5–9 *183*
3:6 *67*
3:6–9 *68*
4:1–2 *127*
9:1–27 *138*
9:16 *104*
9:19–23 *184*
11:26 *103*
12:3 *183*
12:8–10 *132, 133*
12:13 *30*
12–14 *184*
12:28 *133*

14:33 *151, 155*
15:9–10 *183*

2 Corinthians
1:22 *31*
2:6–7 *155*
2:11 *146, 155*
5:11 *105*
5:14 *105*
9:8 *137*
9:22–23 *113*
10:1–4 *160*
10:1–6 *184*
11:13–15 *151*
12:9 *183*

Galatians
3:26–29 *183*
3:27–29 *40*
4:4 *117*
6:1 *33*
6:1–10 *184*

Ephesians
1:13 *31*
2:1–3 *157*
4:1–16 *133*
4:7–13 *132*
4:11–16 *183*
4:26 *154*
4:27 *149, 154*
5:11 *149*
5:18 *30*
6:1–10 *184*
6:10–13 *149*
6:10–20 *160*
6:12 *145*
6:14–20 *149*

Philippians
1:6 *31*
1:12 *87*
2:9–11 *118*

Colossians
3:14 *183*

1 Thessalonians
1:9 *105*
2:4–8 *105*

2 Thessalonians
3:1 *183*

1 Timothy
6:10 *154*

2 Timothy
2:1 *33*
2:2 *53*
4:5 *184*
4:11 *60*

Hebrews
12:1–2 *56*

1 Peter
1:1–2 *71*
1:3–5 *31*
1:10 *71*
3:15 *87, 101*
4:9 *138*
4:9–11 *133*

1 John
2:1 *158*
2:15 *184*
4:4 *147*

Jude
3 *101*
6 *152*

Revelation
2:18 *84*
12:10 *158*
12:11 *103*
12:12 *159*